STEERING THE SHIP TO THE SHORE

Guide for Founders Navigating Startup Waters

SRINI RAJAM

STARDOM BOOKS
www.StardomBooks.com

STARDOM BOOKS

A Division of Stardom Alliance
112 Bordeaux Ct. Coppell,
TX 75019, USA

FIRST EDITION MAY 2023

STARDOM BOOKS

A Division of Stardom Alliance
112 Bordeaux Ct. Coppell,
TX 75019, USA

www.stardombooks.com

Stardom Books, United States
Stardom Alliance, India

STEERING THE SHIP TO THE SHORE

Srini Rajam

p. 150
cm. 13.5 X 21.5

Category:
BUS025000 - Business & Economics:
Entrepreneurship
BUS107000 - Business & Economics: Personal
Success

ISBN: 978-1-957456-22-5

DEDICATION

I dedicate this book to my mother,
(Late) Lakshmi Rajam,
who meant everything to me in my life.

CONTENTS

FOREWORD

There has never been a better time to be an entrepreneur in India as our country is poised to make great strides for many decades to come. Thanks to my experiences as an entrepreneur, mentor, and investor, I have had the privilege of witnessing the remarkable growth of startups over the years. I have also seen many promising ventures falter or fail, often due to the lack of a clear roadmap to success. That's why I am thrilled to introduce you to Srini Rajam's new book, "Steering the Ship to the Shore".

In this practical and compelling guide, Srini shares his insights into navigating the turbulent waters of the startup world. Drawing from his own successful entrepreneurial journey and vast interactions with industry peers and aspiring entrepreneurs, Srini offers an invaluable compass for those looking to steer their startup ships to desired destinations. Those destinations meet the aspirations of all the stakeholders in the journey, viz., the startup team members, investors, and customers. The book gives due importance to the voice of everyone on board the startup journey.

What sets "Steering the Ship to the Shore" apart from other books in the genre is its unique blend of real-world case studies, actionable strategies, and recommendations tailored specifically for the needs of today's startup founders. Srini covers critical aspects of the startup journey, purpose and dream, working with investors, solving customer problems, planning & executing, optimizing funding, rewarding efforts & results, end game options and making conscious efforts to reach home.

One of the aspects I particularly appreciate about the book is Srini's ability to break down complex concepts into easily digestible and actionable steps. Rather than being a text-heavy, theoretical, reference material, this book is a hands-on manual that can be applied to any startup; it's crisp, to-the-point, and full of interesting charts, figures, and step-by-step instructions.

As a friend, I have known Srini for over 25 years from the days of his leadership of Texas Instruments India and co-founding Ittiam with the passion to build an IP focused technology company from India. Srini's actions have demonstrated his commitment to excellence, innovation and knowledge sharing widely in the tech community. I can say with confidence that this book is another testament to that passion and dedication.

I wholeheartedly recommend "Steering the Ship to the Shore" to any startup founder seeking a clear path to success, as well as to practicing entrepreneurs, investors, and mentors who want to sharpen their skills and deepen their understanding of the startup ecosystem. In the pages of this book, you will find the tools, inspiration, and guidance to make your startup journey a successful and fulfilling one.

Happy reading and may your startup ship sail smoothly towards its preferred harbor!

Sincerely,
Nandan Nilekani
Co-Founder and Chairman of Infosys Limited,
Founding Chairman of UIDAI

ACKNOWLEDGMENTS

I want to acknowledge my journey with Texas Instruments (TI) with admiration and fondness. TI's exemplary organizational culture and inspiring leaders have laid the foundation for my professional career. Among several leaders of TI who shaped and guided my thoughts, I would like to especially and sincerely thank Dr. Mohan Rao and Mr. Robert Rozeboom.

It has been an absolute privilege for me to associate with the legend and icon of India's IT industry, Mr. Narayana Murthy, Founder and Former Chairman of Infosys Limited. I have had the opportunity to get his invaluable mentorship for more than two decades since the inception of my entrepreneurial journey with Ittiam.

Ittiam Start-Up Leadership Team 2001

Standing L to R:
Andrew Bhagyanathan, Ravishankar Ganesan, Shantanu Jha, Sattam Dasgupta, Vikram Bose

Sitting L to R:
Rohit Bhuva, Srini Rajam

It has been a dream to be a part of the startup leadership team of Ittiam. I'm so grateful for all my fellow team members, Andrew, Ravi, Rohit, Sattam, Shantanu, and Vikram. We immensely enjoyed working together and learning from each other to establish the long-term foundation for the success of Ittiam.

My startup aspiration originates from (Late) V G Siddhartha, Founder of Coffee Day Enterprises and Head of Global Technology Ventures. He supported Ittiam with great passion through his investment and guiding thoughts. He always held Ittiam's interests on top of his mind and forged the most cherished friendship.

My colleague and Chief Business Officer at Ittiam, Mukund Srinivasan, has opened my eyes to the agility and innovation with which we can create success in the technology industry. Working with him on our strategies and transformations over the past decade has been a pleasure.

Preface

If you appreciate sports as much as I do, for the entertainment value and insights into life, the below-mentioned observation may have crossed your mind.

Soccer and Tennis are two very fascinating sports to watch. Each has its own dynamics and distinctive characteristics. Yet this key difference between them is valuable when considering the start-up world. In Soccer, the team that is in possession of the ball at the end of the match or the team that scored the last goal does not necessarily win the game. It could be the opponent who wins, or the match could end in a draw when the final whistle goes up. However, in Tennis, the player must win the last match point to win the game. The player who scores the last (final) point wins the game. It's not over until the match is over. Even if a team is badly placed at some stage, they will ultimately win the game if they keep scoring on every opportunity they get. In the *World of Tennis*, as long as you are playing and surviving, there is hope that keeps pushing you to fight for the next point, the later point, and so on, to win the match. As a contrast, in the *World of Soccer*, the team trailing heavily towards the end of the game does not have a way to claw back.

Start-ups need to imbibe this *Spirit of Tennis*. There are going to be many lows in the start-up journey. Still, entrepreneurs must not lose hope to achieve the desired outcome by sticking to the game, maintaining laser focus, and winning every new moment.

We have brought this book to uphold this sense of hope in an entrepreneur. This book's content has been segregated into three parts, as illustrated in the diagram below. It comprises The Ship (Start-up), The Steering (Leadership), and The Shore (Home). We have a bonus feature that we call The Lighthouse. The Lighthouse provides the vantage point of view and insights into the start-up ocean where the reader can feel the pulse and mood of startups in different stages of their lifecycle. With this book, we expect our readers to understand the essence of the startup world in fulfilling the aspirations of everyone involved in it and help the readers take a step closer to living their start-up dreams.

Steering the Ship to the Shore

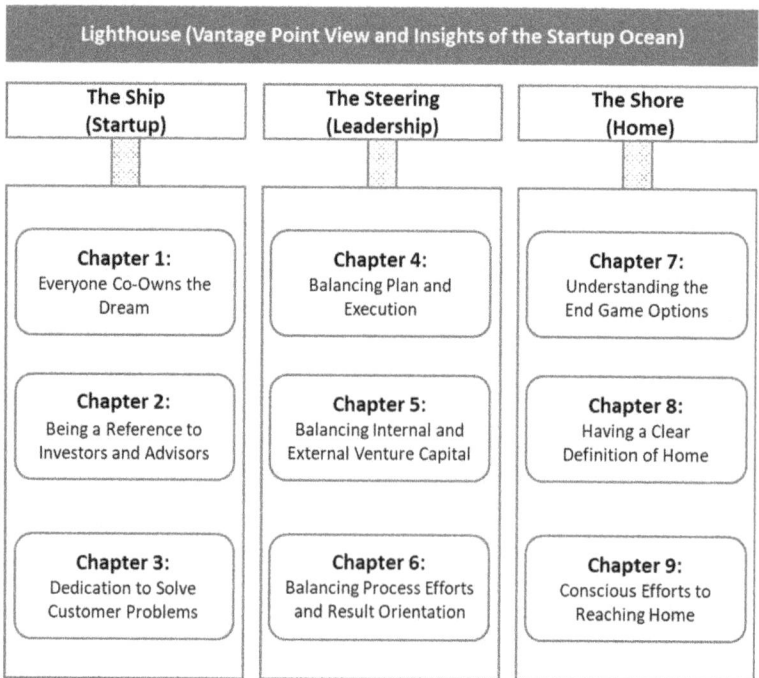

Lighthouse (Vantage Point View and Insights of the Startup Ocean)		
The Ship (Startup)	**The Steering (Leadership)**	**The Shore (Home)**
Chapter 1: Everyone Co-Owns the Dream	**Chapter 4:** Balancing Plan and Execution	**Chapter 7:** Understanding the End Game Options
Chapter 2: Being a Reference to Investors and Advisors	**Chapter 5:** Balancing Internal and External Venture Capital	**Chapter 8:** Having a Clear Definition of Home
Chapter 3: Dedication to Solve Customer Problems	**Chapter 6:** Balancing Process Efforts and Result Orientation	**Chapter 9:** Conscious Efforts to Reaching Home

Introduction

The Book

Only a tiny percentage of people choose to become entrepreneurs, even though entrepreneurs are essential for the progress of an industry, a nation, and society. Few people choose this path because the entrepreneurial journey is risky and arduous since more than 90% of start-ups fail. Most of them only survive a few years and slowly disintegrate towards non-existence. Often, investments are not fully recovered. Some folks lose their passion while on this journey, yet some leave for better prospects or safer options.

However, this need not be the case. In the excitement of exploring multiple opportunities, the leadership of a start-up must not take their eyes off ensuring a successful closure. It's never too late.

This book shares deep insights into the start-up lifecycle and the wisdom of steering it toward the desired destination or home.

You

As a start-up entrepreneur, you are taking a significant risk in life. In this journey, there would be several moments of uncertainty and instances of not knowing how to guide a start-up to produce results that would meet the objectives of all the stakeholders.

As the leader of a start-up, you have a holistic responsibility that is more significant than just creating a good business. All the participants (stakeholders) in the start-up have joined the venture based on their trust in you. They look up to you to guide the ship to the desired shore. This book provides a framework and tools to understand, define, and keep the end objectives of the start-up firmly on the radar and ensure that an entrepreneur knows which direction is most suitable for them.

The Author

Srini Rajam holds a Master's in Computer Science from the Indian Institute of Science (IISc) and has been elected the Distinguished Alumnus of IISc. Appointed as the youngest Country Managing Director of Texas Instruments India in 1994, he led several intrapreneurship initiatives by creating new product divisions and starting up as the first Technical Marketing Director of Texas Instruments in Asia. Srini Co-founded Ittiam Systems in 2001. Ittiam is one of India's most successful IP (Intellectual Property) design companies that have received global recognition and peer admiration. Srini has led the company as Chairman and CEO since its inception.

The book captures the deep learning and experience gained by Srini throughout his career journey.

1

Everyone Co-Owns the Dream

A start-up dream takes birth in the mind of the founder(s), but it grows naturally to become the dream of everyone in the company. The outsider's view of an entrepreneur, by family and society, has dramatically changed for the better over the past forty years. While this positive trend has been seen globally, the change has been even more pronounced in India.

In the 1980s, being employed by government organizations held the highest prestige due to the job security and status it carried. Gradually in the 1990s, those who were employed by multinational companies or large private Indian enterprises got high respect. Even by the late 1990s and early 2000s, the word entrepreneur was a euphemism for unemployment. It took a lot of effort to convince your best friend to join your startup, let alone invest in your venture. Convincing an investor to fund your ideas or a customer to buy your product was another story. In family gatherings, an entrepreneur's introduction would be considered incomplete in describing what they exactly do, and their aunts or uncles would be on their toes to ask, "Why are you not trying to land a better job?" or "Are you still applying for a job?".

We have witnessed a fabulous transformation in this situation in the past two decades. Campus graduates prefer to join fresh start-ups; professionals are getting bold and are creating their ventures early in their careers; venture capital to support powerful ideas is flowing handsomely. People pursuing such endeavors are looked upon with respect and admiration, at least not with sympathy anymore. A relevant example in this context is of two young engineering managers in a world-leading company's India center. They were at the booming stage of their career prospects within the company, yet they decided to boldly start a new venture based on a product idea. They were confident of the future; they wasted no time to start quickly with a small funding from an angel investor intending to make a prototype fast and secure future funding. In an even earlier stage career example, a few friends who did their undergraduate degree in the same campus in India and then a graduate degree in different world-class institutions in India and the U.S. are getting ready to come together straight after higher education to create a startup. The conventional wisdom has been that a long, solid industry working experience gives entrepreneurs with a strong platform to create a new venture successfully. India's new age entrepreneurs are breaking that mold to start the journey as soon as they can in their late twenties and early thirties. They are giving themselves the time advantage to do multiple startups in their career span or possibly learn from one failed attempt to follow up with multiple successful ventures.

With the remarkable rise in entrepreneurship in the current environment, let us look at the basics of entrepreneurship. Entrepreneurship is a journey that begins with huge excitement and risk. One can expect it to end with great satisfaction and reward, but that does not necessarily always happen. When we come across a shining success story of an entrepreneur or a team of entrepreneurs, it makes us feel elated. For every such instance, there are numerous untold stories of failed start-ups that would make us feel dejected. Surviving through the first three years is the first major filter that many startups do not pass. The next critical filter is showing vitality to remain relevant, valuable, and growing. A small percentage of startups that successfully come through the first filter struggle to go beyond this second filter. A common characteristic of both these types of failure is that they have burnt significant investment capital which will not be recovered. This means some part of the startup, be it external investors, founders, family, or friends who contributed the finances, is badly affected. The symptom that closely adjoins the financial failure is the exodus of people who started the journey for better and safer options. Often, companies receive resumes of job applicants who have tried out a venture in the past and have resorted to getting a job with much lower responsibility than even their earlier employment role before the venture saga.

Hence, when you decide to be an entrepreneur, you must embrace what is coming for you and know that you are choosing to walk a risky and arduous path. It is challenging to predict at the beginning whether success will be achieved; experts have noted that the success rate of new ventures is less than 10 percent. Your finances can take a hit, time with family may get curtailed, and the mental stress will keep rising. You could be infected with the "what-if" bug and worry daily about the possibilities of things going completely wrong with your venture. Your reputation amongst friends and professional circles could be affected. Even if that is not the case and your friends look at the positive side to admire your courage, the turmoil you have experienced in the journey can have a negative impact on your self-confidence and bring down your self-esteem.

So, there must be a strong reason for you to choose to stay on this path, to be an entrepreneur, and to create a start-up. I call that the *Purpose*. There is a constant voice within you that wants you to take this risk, to take this path for a purpose that is greater than the fear of all the possible adversities. The heart wants to take the plunge, but the mind forever analyses the probability of succeeding. One morning, you are determined to quit your current job and start a venture independently, however, you are likely to develop cold feet when you see your kid returning from school in the evening and think of their future. Dilemmas like this are very common and expected.

The purpose becomes the key to breaking the deadlock between your heart's passion and mind's fear. You want to visualize yourself twenty years into the future. What would that version of yourself have liked your present version to have decided? Take the safer option of the status quo and regret the missed opportunity for the rest of your life or give yourself a chance to pursue your heart. Often, if the purpose is genuine, strong, and compelling, this visualization will lead to only one answer.

That will be to start up.

Identify the Purpose

Ask yourself, "What is the purpose for which I am more than willing to take on the huge risk and adversity?" The purpose is something personal to you. It could be the freedom that entrepreneurship creates-or becoming a pioneer in your family, professional community or even the nation. It could be the unique recognition that it would bring to you. It may even be the personal commitment that you have made to someone most dear and close.

Here are some of the commonly cited purposes by experienced and aspiring entrepreneurs. There could also be some other purposes that enrich this list.

- Freedom
- To be a Pioneer
- Excitement
- Satisfaction
- Recognition
- Reward
- Fulfilling a Commitment

Whatever your purpose, make sure to print that single word (or phrase) in bold letters and pin it over your workspace. This is because, along the journey as an entrepreneur, you may face extremely difficult moments where you could be left wondering why I am here and whose idea it is. You then want to glance at the pinboard to reassure and re-dedicate yourself. The purpose is the reason you want to wake up every day from now on.

For example, your purpose is freedom, and you value it greater than anything else. So, you are ready to make the sacrifices of longer working hours and lesser financial affordability that may come with it.

Your purpose could be satisfaction, and you willingly relinquished an executive job and big title to roll up your sleeves and get onto the working field to do what you enjoy.

I had my purpose that broke the deadlock whether I should be an entrepreneur or not. Once I identified it, the decision appeared so straightforward. I will describe it shortly in the next section along with a closely allied concept called *Dream*.

Purpose Leads to the Dream

Purpose leads to *a dream*, a visualization of what you want to create or where you want to go. You dream of something not there now, but you want to make it happen in the future. It is a dream because it is exhilarating, something you cannot just buy at the stores; something that will not happen by itself in the natural course of time.

Purpose and dream are both high-level forces. They have one crucial difference.

Whereas purpose is a personal attribute, the dream can be and should become a collective attribute of all the people who will come together on the journey. Several people can be driven by different purposes individually, but they share a common dream.

Since the dream must appeal to many people, it must have a significance that will relate to and inspire all of them. It exists for the greater good and happiness of everyone.

A personal illustration will help relate to the distinction between purpose and dream. The company I co-founded in 2001 called Ittiam Systems has been built on a dream (described soon following this) that brought all the people together. However, even before thinking of the dream, I had a personal purpose that drove me to become an entrepreneur. At that time, I was in the sixth year of my tenure as the Managing Director of Texas Instruments India. This global technology giant has been widely credited with pioneering the hi-tech revolution in India. It was one of the most active and prestigious phases of my career.

As much as I enjoyed it, the next career step was looming. My next logical assignment in the Texas Instruments World was to relocate to the company's headquarters in Dallas, Texas, U.S., to take up new responsibilities. However, remaining in India and continuing to live with my mother was a much bigger purpose in my life for which I was ready to take on the risk and explore out-of-the-box options. The power of my purpose made it so easy for me to choose the path of entrepreneurship.

Our other co-founders of Ittiam similarly had their personal purposes, but our dream was common and uniting as described herein.

Incidentally, the name Ittiam was a brilliant spark created in our founding team conversations. It is the acronym of the world-famous quote by the French Philosopher and Mathematician Rene Descartes "I Think Therefore I Am". In his respect, the premier conference room of our company is named Descartes, where we hold important customer and company board meetings. Of course, Rene Descartes' words convey the power of dreaming and thinking in shaping one's life and existence. The impact of giving such an inspiring name to our start-up was immense. Anyone to whom we introduced the company to would remember its name and origin. "Wow, that's so wonderful and thoughtful, I will remember it" was the typical reaction that followed the introduction.

The Ittiam (I Think Therefore I Am) Dream

The dream that was pervasive in the minds of us in the founding team of Ittiam was to *"Build a World Class Technology Product Company from India."*

What was the significance of that dream, and why did it attract more people towards it?

EVERYONE CO-OWNS THE DREAM

Ittiam was founded in Bangalore, India, on New Year's Day of 2001, the first day of the New Millennium. It turned out that our dream was a harbinger of the aspirations and confidence of new India.

In the 1980s, Indian technology was known to the world through the outstanding achievements of Indian-origin scientists, technologists and engineers who moved out of the country to the U.S. and other parts of the world.

In the 1990s, India's technological prowess was showcased to the world through the research and development centres set up by multinational giants such as Texas Instruments and globally successful Indian software services companies such as Infosys and Wipro.

The founders of Ittiam came with extensive experience in enacting the famed story of Texas Instruments in India. They carried the dream to extend India's technology advancement to the next frontier, i.e., to build India's own world-class technology product company. Such a compelling and relatable dream attracted everyone with whom the dream was shared. For the first 20 engineering positions advertised in the newspapers, more than 10,000 prospective engineers applied within the first week. Proposals for venture capital investment into the company poured in from Indian and overseas investors.

Everyone who was part of Ittiam, not just the founders, made the dream their own and wanted to make it a reality. They expressed their ownership of the dream through their words and actions.

Share the Dream and Make Everyone Co-Own It

A great dream created within one mind or the minds of a small team of people has the potential to find resonance with a much larger team of players who could become a part of it. There are many opportunities and avenues for that dream to be shared collectively.

Your dream is best shared through personalized interaction and experience. To state it emphatically using the contrary, an email broadcast is not the way to share your dream. Coffee table chats, off-site events, and workshops managed with the help of expert consultants are a few excellent approaches to do it.

Sharing the dream involves conveying the story, emotions, and significance, which form the essential backdrop. It requires personal time for everyone. You can start with the start-up's small team of founders and senior leaders. You can then take it broader within the group. The test of effective sharing is that the recipients make the dream their own and become the spokespersons to share it further from their hearts. This is a slow percolation process, much like how the iconic filter coffee is made in some parts of India, whose output quality is unmatched by other instant coffee-making methods.

At the end of this deliberate process, you get everyone on the same page regarding the dream.

The simple phrase or sentence that describes the dream is recalled anytime, anywhere, and by anyone associated with the start-up. It comes out of their heart.

Here is an illustration of sharing the dream from the first few days of Ittiam. We held an offsite event on a lovely evening in Bangalore with the first batch of 20 "Ittians", engineers who joined the company from more than 10,000 aspiring applicants. What made the event special was that the parents, relatives, and friends of the engineers were also invited. It was an opportunity to meet, greet and get to know each other. The founders spoke about the Ittiam dream and what the company is setting out to do along with the new recruits. The impact of the event was revealed in the subsequent days when many of the engineers spoke about how impressed their parents were about the Ittiam dream and proud of their sons and daughters joining such an organization.

Having the dream resident not only in the minds of a few founders but also in the minds of everyone in the company is a significant differentiation for attracting and developing talent. It is common knowledge that we live in an ultra-competitive era where every talented professional has multiple job and career choices. Just as companies select the candidate to hire, the candidate is selecting the company to work for. People choose to be a part of an organization whose dream aligns best with their principles. You want to share the dream with the prospective team members to help them make an informed decision.

Articulate the Vision

As already noted, purpose and dream are higher-level themes. With them in place, we now move to the next level of describing what the start-up business is all about or, in other words, its vision. In fact, from the given purpose and dream can flow multiple visions.

The purpose is the force that is personal and remains a constant.

The dream is the visualization of the future that is common to everyone.

Vision is one specific instance of a dream. Vision can have relevance for a specific time, say, five years. It can evolve with time. Over a decade or more, the start-up can pursue multiple visions to realize the dream and serve the individual purposes of the people involved. The graphic in Fig. 1.1 helps to understand these three concepts and their distinctions.

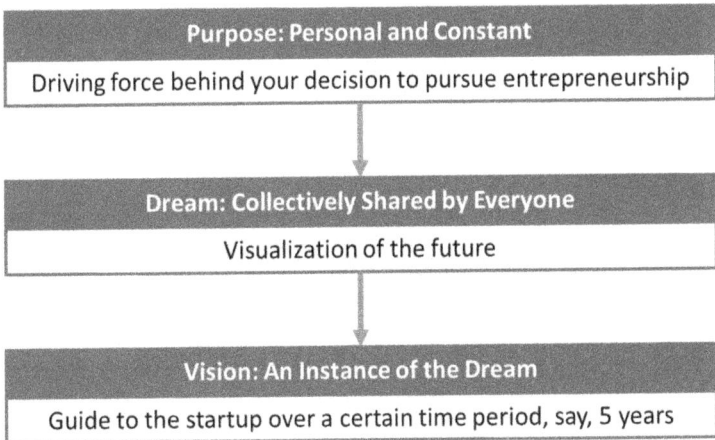

| Purpose: Personal and Constant |
| Driving force behind your decision to pursue entrepreneurship |

| Dream: Collectively Shared by Everyone |
| Visualization of the future |

| Vision: An Instance of the Dream |
| Guide to the startup over a certain time period, say, 5 years |

Fig. 1.1: Purpose, Dream and Vision

The vision statement that guided Ittiam in its first phase was to be a *"World Leader in Digital Signal Processing Systems"*. Comparing this statement with the Dream, you can notice that the broader phrase "Technology Product Company" has been given the specific instance of "Digital Signal Processing Systems", which represented one of the foundational technologies of the early 21st century. It was the basis for digital communications, on-demand entertainment, and the digital media revolution, transforming the world since the early 2000s. So, we matched the dream with an equally compelling vision.

Full Scope of Start-up Co-Ownership and Stakeholders' Spectrum

So far, we have viewed the dream's co-ownership from the perspective of the founders and people on the start-up team. This is the first important step involving people directly inside the company. Who are the other key people who must own the company's dream and have a stake in its success?

The people inside the company envision the future and work hard to realize it. To do this successfully, they need the support of two important external constituents who must also become stakeholders – Investors / Advisors and Customers / Partners. For simplicity, we will represent the full set of "Investors and Advisors" with the term "Investors", and the full set of "Customers and Partners" with the term "Customers".

While we will consider the perspectives of Investors and Customers in depth in the next two chapters, the summary lines here will be helpful to understand the concept of Stakeholders' Spectrum in this chapter. Investors facilitate the start-up to access the financial resources necessary to run the company. Customers provide the ultimate meaning for what the start-up creates by being the company's users (of the products and services) and source of revenue. When the co-ownership is extended to bring in the key external stakeholders of Investors and Customers, we create a well-rounded Stakeholders' Spectrum as illustrated in Fig. 1.2. The three constituents come together to complete the structure, as we will see further in the following two chapters of Part I of The Ship (Start-up). The start-up must add unique, relevant and meaningful value to each stakeholder in the spectrum. We will build this structure further as we go along in this book to understand it closely.

What top values can the start-up deliver to the People, Investors and Customers? The Stakeholders' Spectrum has placeholders for two of them, marked as "Value-1" and "Value-2". There could be more values, but we show two of them here in this illustration. The "Value-1" for People is shown based on this chapter's description, which is to deliver "Co-Ownership". You can consider the possible "Value-2" for people in your start-up.

It may be the opportunity to work in cutting-edge technology areas you are engaged in. It may be the fast pace of learning your environment enables. It could be the benchmark compensation and rewards, although you know as well as anyone that it is a super hard and moving goalpost!

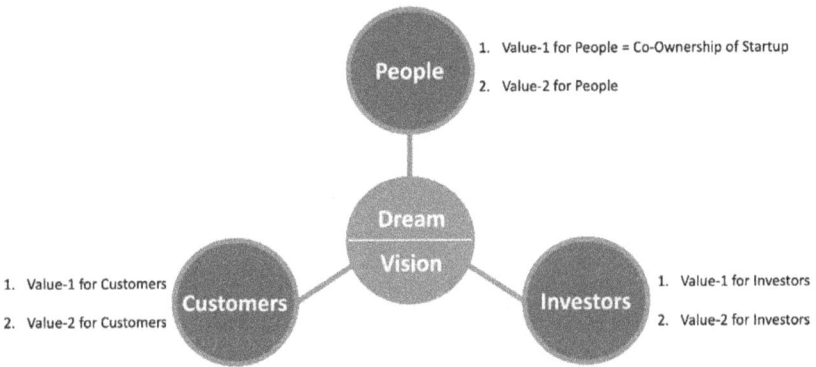

People

1. Value-1 for People = Co-Ownership of Startup
2. Value-2 for People

Dream

Vision

Customers

1. Value-1 for Customers
2. Value-2 for Customers

Investors

1. Value-1 for Investors
2. Value-2 for Investors

Fig. 1.2: Co-Owners of the Dream

The Ship in the Context of the Steering and the Shore

Let us now analyze the metaphor 'ship'; we look at the ship in detail since it is foundational to the book's overall theme and vital to the two parts to follow which deal with the steering and the shore. It is useful to note here that the "shore" represents a home or success for the start-up that is very important in a given time window. Over a much longer time scale, the shore itself can transform from one type to another. The start-up making an IPO (Initial Public Offering) to be listed in a stock exchange is a fine example of shore. Other examples include being acquired by a large company or merging with a partner company.

The stakeholders' spectrum that makes up the ship needs to be harmonious, energetic, and positive. That will be the basis on which critical decisions and trade-offs in the steering phase will be made and implemented. It will also be instrumental for the entire team to have a clear understanding and consensus of the shore (home) to be reached.

We are now ready to take a deeper look into the investors and customers as stakeholders in the following two chapters.

Top Three Takeaways (T3)

1. Your purpose in pursuing entrepreneurship is the driver for everything that follows. Introspect deeply and identify it clearly. Do not rush this phase. This is personal to you.

2. Understand the distinction and relationship among Purpose, Dream, and Vision. Document them precisely with the help of the template in Fig. 1.1 which is reproduced here below for your chapter notes.

3. The stakeholders' spectrum spanning People, Investors, and Customers in Fig. 1.2 must always remain on the radar. The values in that chart will be filled up as we build the spectrum further.

Purpose is your personal attribute.

Dream is a collective attribute of everyone joining you on the startup journey.

A Light-Bulb Moment in Chapter-1

Purpose: Personal and Constant

↓

Dream: Collectively Shared by Everyone

↓

Vision: An Instance of the Dream

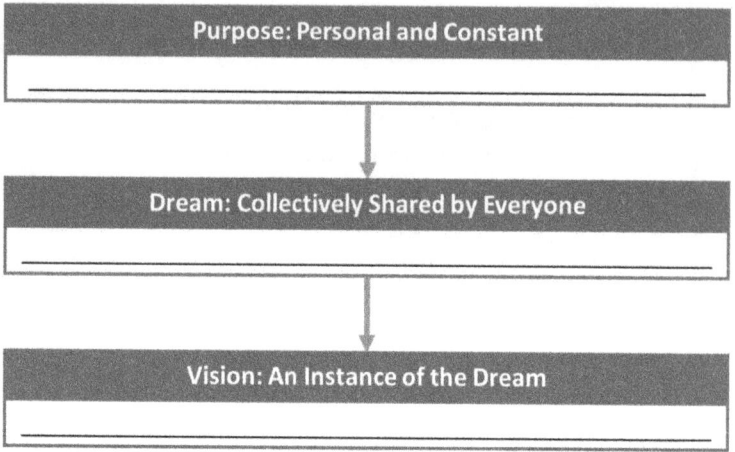

For Your T3 Notes from Chapter 1

2

Being a Reference to Investors and Advisors

A start-up not only benefits from the investment and guidance from investors and advisors, but it can also, in turn, benefit them by being a shining example that they would be proud to showcase as a reference of their success.

In its beginning, the start-up is a new and unknown idea, perhaps almost an alien concept to begin a career journey. It has some essential credibility from its founders' track record and reputation if they have prior start-up experience or have played crucial roles in large corporations. Some successful entrepreneurs create new start-ups once they exit their previous ventures, which brings instant credibility to the new start-up since "they have been there, done it, and can very likely do it again."

The essential reputation is enhanced by the quality of people joining the start-up and, ultimately, by its output. In the early stage of a start-up, people are attracted and inducted through professional networks that cut across companies and countries and word-of-mouth references from mentors they respect. Investors and advisors, whom we focus on in this chapter, also play a significant role in this process.

First and foremost, investors are needed for an exceptional reason. They provide the financial capital required for the start-up to manage itself and create a good runway for the business to take off. In addition to this core value, investors can help the start-up with key references and connections in the global business network.

The value of the reference you can get from a proven and respected leader in the industry cannot be emphasized sufficiently. It opens doors to places that would otherwise take a very long time to get to or even be impossible to reach. Of course, that leader must know you and be confident to provide the reference. A thumb rule of how well you are connected within your industry is whether you are within 2-hops to every key person you want to reach out to. Even if you may not know that person directly (one hop), you are close to someone else who could provide that introduction (two hops). Of course, this is a network you develop over time and experience, and it is okay if you need more than two hops, especially early in your career.

Advisors add exceptional value too. Based on their deep expertise and vast experience in their field, they can offer guidance to the start-up that could be pivotal for future success. In another dimension, their advice could help the start-up avoid making a big mistake that would result in losing valuable time, resources, and money. So, advisors can both enable smart decisions and help avoid costly blunders.

From the early days of the start-up being known by its investors and advisors, the direction of imparting credibility can later take a pleasant 180-degree turn when the start-up becomes successful.

Investors and investment companies are part of a larger process and objective of growing the value of the financial capital they manage. They want to produce the best return on their investment that they can. Their investment portfolio can contain several asset classes of differing risk and return potential. Start-ups present the high-risk and high-return model, a necessary element in the overall portfolio.

Investors will want to showcase their investment if the start-up grows and succeeds. That would be a proof point to enhance their credibility of creating successful companies of the future and attracting more start-ups to work with them. This is quite like a graduate student being known by the top-tier university they get into. Later, the same university showcases them as their famous alumni when the student achieves outstanding success in their profession and life.

For example, even Google was a new start-up kid on the block in 1998, looking for its initial investors to provide funding and add credibility. Eventually, as one of the world's largest, most powerful, and most highly influential technology corporations it has since become, Google (now part of the holding company Alphabet) has, in turn, enhanced the credibility of its original investors many folds more significantly than what it received from them.

Articulating the Start-up's Value to Investors and Advisors

When a start-up is pitching to a prospective investor, some fundamental aspects are evaluated, such as the Market Opportunity, Product Differentiation, Business Plan, People Capability, and Return on Investment (ROI). Stating modestly, it does help if the start-up exhibits the potential that one of the benefits of investing in it is the possibility of the start-up becoming an excellent reference to the investor in its successful future version. The same principle holds good for attracting advisors to the start-up as well.

During prospective investment meetings, exhibiting the start-up's potential for becoming a reference need not be done explicitly or flamboyantly. It can be through subtle communication from the start-up and inferred conclusion from the investor. For example, the start-up pitch could talk about the plans to attain global market leadership in its product which would naturally present a future opportunity for the investor to refer to such a success. In a different scenario, there could be key technology connections and synergies between the start-up's offerings and the needs of a few other companies in the investor's investment portfolio. Highlighting these opportunities while describing the industry partnership strategy of the start-up would serve as a natural reminder to the investor of the cross-investment leverage they can derive by working with the start-up being assessed now.

The investor welcomes the quietly confident and self-assured entrepreneur. Initially, the start-up is new and gains by the induction of a proven investor, but in due course, the payback can happen the other way around.

Key Elements of a Start-up in Investor Assessment

The important factors about a start-up that would be assessed in investment decisions vary from investor to investor. We come across some interestingly unique factors being prioritized by marquee investors.

For example, geographical proximity to the start-up and management team was a surprising factor gathered from one investor conversation. It was about investing in start-ups in the local neighborhood or ecosystem. Their logic was sound in that they believe in close collaboration and face-to-face interaction as the key to guiding the start-up toward success. They were not interested in start-ups that were thousands of miles or many hours of time zones away, even though they understood and appreciated those start-ups' quality and business viability.

In another case, the critical factor was that the minimum investment size must be above a significant threshold, such as USD 25 million. It was linked to their investment philosophy to take a few larger bets than many smaller ones. It was also based on the rationale that the investor's management bandwidth allocated for a start-up is roughly the same regardless of the investment size. Hence it is better to focus on a few extensive opportunities than many smaller ones, each of which takes away the same effort and time from the investor's perspective.

An inverse function of the size factor applied by some investors is to prioritize start-ups that require investment below a modest threshold, such as USD 2 million, and those with an opportunity to co-invest a smaller amount with other leading investors. On the lower side of this size dimension, some angel investors look to limit their exposure to less than half a million dollars to get things started and let more prominent institutional investors drive the subsequent investments. Their logic is to spread the bet wider, learn from a broad set of experiences and limit the downward risk in any of them. It is also likely that these investors are operating within a relatively smaller capital (Fund Under Management) and hence cannot invest large capital in a single start-up.

After seeing some prominently different investment factors, one possibly constant factor in investment decisions, regardless of the start-up and investor combinations, is the importance of the founding team. *"We bet on people rather than one particular idea"* is a refrain commonly heard from the investment fraternity. The principle here is that intelligent people will not only come up with a great idea but will also adapt it to be a more appropriate idea should the dynamic market environment demand a change. So rather than betting on one winning formula, they bet on the people who know how to win. They like people knowing to fish rather than those having the fish for the day. To illustrate this point, the Android operating system, which today powers more than 70+% as of May 2023 data of smartphones worldwide, was initially conceived in its venture to create an operating system for smart cameras. A very timely and intelligent pivot into targeting the immense potential of mobile handsets had set the product roadmap onto a path of becoming one of the most influential technology platforms in the world today. While remaining firmly committed to the start-up's overarching Purpose, Dream and Vision, the management's ability to adapt the product strategy to the dynamically evolving market opportunities is an important attribute of successful start-ups.

Before opening discussions with prospective investors, a proper homework that a start-up can do is to prepare a self-assessment table of how the start-up would rate against several typical factors of importance to investors. This table can contain a superset of factors, even though not all may be considered necessary by a given investor. Also, the weightage (or priority) assigned by Investor-A to a factor could be quite different from the weightage assigned by Investor-B to the same factor. Even allowing for such variations, this self-assessment table is a good homework that enables the start-up with a proper baseline to approach the investors and be well prepared for the discussions.

An illustrative framework of such a self-assessment table is provided in Fig. 2.1. You can treat this as a live document with which you can create the first version and upgrade it based on actual investor conversations and learnings. This table can be maintained with different versions at different timelines and situations of your start-up lifecycle, providing a structured reference to study the past before taking up any future discussion.

Here are helpful notes to understand the illustrative self-assessment table in Fig 2.1 and use it more broadly across various prospective investor discussions.

Key Factor of Investment	Importance Rating for Investor (Min 1 to Max 10)	Self-Assessment Rating by Startup (Min 1 to Max 10)	Remarks
Qualitative Factors			
Trust with Founding Team	10		
Alignment of Startup Vision with Investor Philosophy	10		Startup and Investor on the same page with their vision and strategy
Track Record of Founding Team	8		
Quantitative Factors			
Legal Due Diligence Clearance	10		
5-Year | 7-Year ROI Potential	10		
Options for Investment Exit	10		
Market Addressed by the Startup	8		
Quality of the Business Plan	8		
Growth Potential of Startup	8		Investor trade off between growth and profitability in early phase
Profitability of Startup	6		
Startup's Ability to Raise Further Capital for Subsequent Phases	5		
Opportunity to Co-Invest and More Validation of Due Diligence	5		

Fig. 2.1: Illustrative Self-Assessment Table of Startup From Investor Perspective

The table lists the factors under two broad categories, qualitative and quantitative. The qualitative factors shown in this illustration relate to trust, alignment of philosophies and track record of the founder(s).

These factors are soft but equally important as the quantitative factors that can be supported with hard data. Even when the quantitative factors are yet to be entirely determined due to work-in-progress or lack of reliable data, the qualitative factors help to get an in-principle green signal from the investor's viewpoint to proceed with the assessment.

In the above illustration, the quantitative factors with the highest importance (rating of 10) prioritize the legally clear start-up, has strong Return on Investment (ROI) potential, and provides practically feasible exit options. Such a priority is common to be expected. The importance of business plan quality cannot be emphasized enough. We will see this in more detail in the fourth chapter.

Investors typically look to trade-off between growth and profitability potential in the early stages of the start-up. There are outlier scenarios of this trade-off where specific business models exclusively focus on growing to acquire an extensive customer base (number of users or subscribers), enabling much larger strategic initiatives to be undertaken. Hence it should not come as a surprise to be sitting in investment discussions where the focus for the short-term is primarily growth and the potential losses incurred to achieve that growth are considered fine by the investor. However, this should not be misunderstood to think that profitability is unimportant. On the contrary, that is one of the most important factors for sustained long-term viability of a start-up. It is only a matter of time before that jumps to the top of review radar and it is in the start-up's best interest to retain focus on it all the time.

Paramount Importance of Trust

We will spend a little time on the qualitative factor of Trust discussed in the investment assessment.

Trust is paramount for every relationship with investors, customers, partners, people within the start-up, or any other external organization. This is such a foundational and broadly applicable factor. While we devote some attention to it here, its relevance must be understood as pervasive to all aspects of the start-up without exception.

Successful and long-term relationships are built on trust. In turn, trust is built on integrity. If there is one quality that you never want to compromise, this must be it.

People are naturally happy and comfortable working with those who share similar views. People are fine to work with those with different perspectives but are upfront about it. However, people want to only work with those they can trust. So, if you want to work with people and want them to work with you, trust is the currency.

There are real-world actions and events by which trust grows positively or erodes negatively. We can look at a few examples to understand this process from which it would be easy to visualize how it works.

It paves the most robust platform to build trust when you demonstrate consistency between your thoughts, words, and actions while interfacing with others. Conversely, the inconsistencies you exhibit make you less trustworthy. Since we are in the chapter on investors, you can see how this relates directly to the trust factor in the start-up investment assessment. If you don't know the answer to a question, the best solution is to say so honestly. When you overpromise and under-deliver, the investor may, at best, give you a second chance, after which they will no longer trust you. The relationship is broken at that point and repairing it will be a steep climb in time and effort. Sometimes it would not be possible at all.

Trust grows when you show empathy in your interaction with the other person. The trust level will jump if you can go one step further and help them beyond the strict call of duty. The other person appreciates that you are not in it just for a one-off transaction but are genuinely trying to build a long-term relationship. They reciprocate. Each one takes the other person's words at total face value and believes in the other. They make big decisions together and care for each other's success.

The saying *'actions speak louder than words'* applies perfectly to the topic of trust we discuss in this section. In the two examples above, you can demonstrate that you do what you say, and are truly committed to the success of a partnership in good times and in adverse conditions.

Investor Dialog is a 2-Way Evaluation Process.

In approaching the investor dialog, you would want to be clear that there is a well-balanced equation. Not only is the investor evaluating the start-up to decide on investing, but also the start-up evaluating the investor to decide on accepting the investment. As noted in the first chapter, the investor will become more than just a financial partner to the start-up, they will become a part of the stakeholders' spectrum.

Hence discussion with prospective investors presents a perfect opportunity to share your dream. A shared dream can lead to the desired outcome of the dream becoming co-owned. This seamlessly extends the stakeholder group from founders and team members to investors. The dreams may only sometimes match. Let us say a start-up is passionate about achieving something which does not match the investor's philosophy. Both parties should agree to disengage the communications. Understanding the differences earlier than later in the collaboration is much better for everyone involved. There is nothing right or wrong in each party's view, just that they are not made for coming together.

Start-ups typically like to secure investors who offer the best valuation of the company (we will see the valuation factor in more detail in Chapter 5). While valuation is essential, it should not become the predominant factor. In addition to keeping valuation on the radar, close alignment and matching of dreams must play a vital role in this decision. The same principle would apply to bringing advisors on board.

Continuing with the illustration of our company Ittiam Systems, we were fortunate to have had many investment opportunities and interests to work with. The investment community is closely-knit. If one of them were to rate your start-up as a bright star, a few others would likely come to know of it, and you would soon be getting a call from them too.

The first investor who came on board of Ittiam, provides an apt example of the principles shared here.

Story of GTV (Global Technology Ventures) Investment in Ittiam

When Ittiam was about to be established, the founders' track record and their potential attracted many prospective investors from India and abroad.

Among them, Ittiam found its dream resonating perfectly with the Chairman of Global Technology Ventures (GTV) Group, (Late) Mr V G Siddhartha. GTV later became a part of his Cafe Coffee Day (CCD) Group of Enterprises.

In the late 1990s, GTV and Siddhartha had already invested in India's software service companies. They were looking to venture into the Technology Product space, and Ittiam's dream also became theirs. Such a close alignment not only helped with the initial decisions of both parties but during many critical moments along the way in deciding on new technologies and business opportunities to diversify into.

True to the title of this chapter, Ittiam became *the technology company* that Mr. Siddhartha and his group would discuss in their industry discussions. In other words, *Ittiam became a reference* to the investor.

Creating Visibility Towards Becoming a Reference

When the start-up gains visibility and recognition in the industry, it naturally helps to be the reference for its investors and advisors, which can be considered a distinction.

However, this visibility creation should differ from Public Relations (PR), expensive advertisement programs, and paid media promotions.

On the other hand, the most reputed visibility you can gain is through third-party acknowledgments and neutral publications appreciating the start-up's work. For example, when the start-up wins a globally acclaimed industry award, it speaks volumes than what advertorial pages can do. The respect the start-up enjoys in leading campuses and with aspiring students is a valuable yardstick. When independent benchmarks rate the start-up's products highly, the visibility rises genuinely. Such forums should be the focus for creating accurate visibility rather than dedicated PR campaigns.

Sharing the Dream and Vision with Customers

As we have seen in this chapter, there is every possibility of the start-up being able to attract a top investor on its potential of becoming an excellent reference for the investor. Nothing succeeds like success, and success has many fathers. A start-up's success makes it a perfect reference for everyone associated with it.

Winning customers is one fundamentally important aspect which everyone concurs as the basis for success. The story and the dream must also be shared with the customers since they make the final pillar of the stakeholder structure. The "Start-up Ship" is complete with bringing the customers on board, leading us to the next chapter.

Building the Stakeholders' Spectrum

In Chapter 1, we looked at the stakeholders' spectrum starting with the people and noted that we would build the spectrum further with investors and customers. What are the most important values your start-up can add to the investor?

From the discussion in this chapter, being a reference is a crucial value and differentiation you can add to the investor. As we also noted, even though the investors' priorities vary from one to another, the ROI (Return on Investment) has universal appeal. The former is from the set of qualitative factors in the self-assessment table shown in Fig. 2.1, and the latter is from the collection of quantitative factors. The spectrum developed further would appear as shown in Fig. 2.2 below. This is, again, illustrative, and you can instantiate it in the most appropriate way for your start-up scenario.

You will also notice that we have filled up "Value-2" for people from the three top candidates discussed in Chapter 1. To recap, those three candidates are: a) Opportunity to work in cutting edge technology, b) Fast paced learning environment and c) Benchmark compensation and reward. The 'learning environment" gets the pick from those strong candidates as shown in our illustration in Fig. 2.2, since it is a relatively more enduring value and more difficult for competition to replicate. You may have already considered what could be the best choice for "Value-2" from your start-up perspective and can update your notes accordingly.

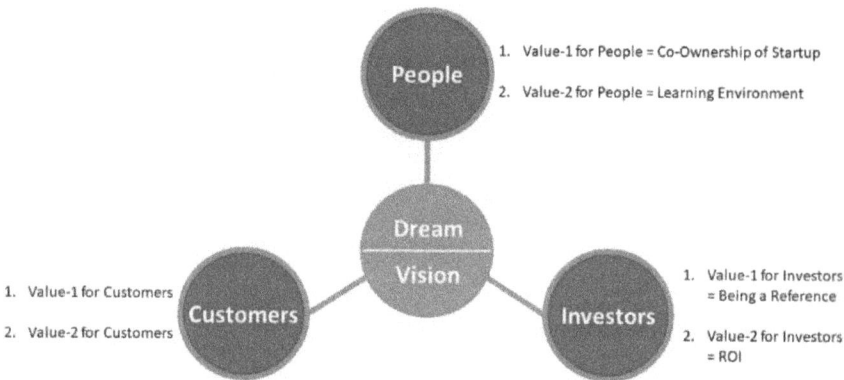

Fig. 2.2: Co-Owners of the Dream

BEING A REFERENCE TO INVESTORS AND ADVISORS

Top Three Takeaways (T3)

1. External investment has become a standard requirement for a modern-day start-up. In addition to providing the financial capital needed for the start-up, investors also help the start-up by being an essential reference. When the start-up grows to be a significant success, it can, in turn, become a quoted reference by the investor.

2. Approach the investment dialog as a 2-way evaluation process. Not only is the investor evaluating you to decide on investing, but so are you evaluating the investor to decide on taking the investment. Alignment and matching of dreams must play a vital role in this decision. Keep the investor selection from being dominated only by the valuation factor.

3. A valuable homework and archive you can create is a self-assessment table of how the start-up would rate against several typical factors of importance to investors. This can be prepared for future investor meetings and maintained with different versions at different timeframes and situations. The archive would provide a structured reference to study the past before taking up any future discussion. Fig. 2.1 provides an illustrative template for this table.

Establish mutual trust between you and the prospective investor.

What you build on that trust will be long-lasting.

A Light-Bulb Moment in Chapter-2

3

Dedication to Solve Customer Problems

Imbibe the spirit "what is the most important problem faced by my customer, how can I provide an efficient solution, and what needs to be done to make my customer succeed?"

Let us begin this chapter with a famous quote on customers attributed to Mahatma Gandhi. An authentic confirmation that he said these words does not exist anywhere in the vast collections of his writings. However, the quote is so powerful and relevant to our subject that we reproduce it here to build upon the concepts further.

> *"A Customer is the most important visitor on our premises.*
> *He is not dependent on us. We are dependent on him.*
> *He is not an interruption to our work. He is the purpose of it.*
> *He is not an outsider to our business. He is a part of it.*
> *We are not doing him a favor by serving him. He is doing us a favor by*
> *allowing us to do so."*

So, how important is the customer for a start-up or any business? The answer would be "utmost import." Some even extend that to say that the customer is the only thing that matters, and everything else can be managed. Interestingly, the words in the quote *"not an outsider but a part of our business"* convey the same spirit that the customer is a part of the stakeholders' spectrum discussed in this book.

When one thinks of any start-up, two immediate questions come to mind: 1) what does the start-up do? and 2) who is the potential customer for what it does?

Marketing experts would even advise processing these questions in the reverse order, i.e., start with (2) first and then work backward to decide on (1).

So, the significance of customers may need no further elaboration. Of course, in this book, we elevate it to the next level by making them one of the three pillars of the start-up structure and stakeholders' spectrum. When you share your vision and dream with the customers and execute the core processes related to customers with perfection, you lay the foundation for successful long-term relationships.

Start-up's Value in the Eyes of the Customer

When prospective customers evaluate a business proposal from a start-up, first and foremost, they are looking to see its capability and commitment to solving their problems not only for the immediate present but also for the long-term future.

Customers are particularly wary of start-ups who may only be around temporarily. This is because start-ups have a high risk of discontinuity in the early years. Even if the start-up were to offer a world-beating solution right now, it's only good if it would last long enough to be of continued value. In this context, a start-up having strong invested capital reserves and investor backing for future financial needs goes a long way in creating confidence with customers about the long-term viability of the start-up. We can see this positive correlation between the two stakeholders, investors and customers, discussed in the previous chapter and this chapter.

In the same spirit of sharing the start-up dream with all its people, investors, and advisors, doing it also with the customers helps to build lasting business relationships, confidence, and trust. When you do this, you pass the first gate in the customer's mind about the start-up lasting long and continuing to support them.

Closely adjoining the continuity gate is the capability gate. Here, the start-up's dedication to understanding and solving customers' problems as its core principle plays a crucial role in its selection to do business with.

Dedication to Solve Customer Problems

You want to take every opportunity to demonstrate to the customer sincerely that the start-up ultimately exists to understand and solve their problems and make them successful.

Fig. 3.1: Dedicated Focus on Solving Customer Problems

The process and key elements embedded in Fig. 3.1 is an excellent template for communicating externally to prospective customers and internally within the team. The process enables you to:

a) Lucidly state the core competencies and capabilities of your start-up.

b) Convey a clear understanding of the customer's problems and the dedication to understanding it better continuously.

c) Express what makes the start-up uniquely placed and differentiated to address customers' problems.

The above approach gives you substantial table stakes to get into the play. The final clincher to win can come from sharing the start-up's dream and vision. Customers find it most reassuring to work with start-ups driven by a dream and vision. You want to demonstrate the commitment to this philosophy in every thought and deed.

Finally, you extend the stakeholders' spectrum by genuinely integrating the customers and their priorities into the start-up.

Customer Problem Understanding is a Multi-Level Initiative

The process captured in the previous section and Fig 3.1 begins with understanding the customer's significant problem(s). It is vital to realize that understanding customer problems is non-trivial and takes a multi-level initiative to accomplish it effectively.

Firstly, the customers you want to work with will not just give a simple notice stating their fundamental problems. It may not be their priority to make such a communication. They could indicate the problems indirectly by describing how they manifest in other issues. Further, some presently emerging and future problems could be even a little unknown to them. So, the problem statement will not be available on a platter. It must be earned through hard work.

Companies invest top dollars and people resources in garnering this market intelligence and keeping it current. As a start-up, you should take the initiative at multiple levels. For one, there is no substitute for facetime with as many current and prospective customers as possible. An essential skill required for this exercise is listening. It can be augmented with collaborative brainstorming. The next significant effort would be playing an active role in class-leading conferences and tradeshows that are directly relevant and at the cutting edge of your domain. Your participation helps to understand the state-of-the-art and shape your future products and solutions with that learning. In the same breadth, participation is also an excellent opportunity to demonstrate your current products and solutions and get live feedback from a wide range of participants.

These initiatives come under the broader classification of the Marketing function. As depicted in Fig. 3.2, marketing encompasses two significant directions. In-to-Out is about going to the market with product promotions and sales. Out-to-In is about listening to the market voice to understand the trends and shape your product strategy. The simple icons convey that the former deals with speaking and the latter with listening. They need to be appreciated in their full scope rather than taken narrowly in that sense.

It is understood that start-ups can only afford to create a few functions and departments. They also operate in a manner where key people multiplex and manage multiple responsibilities at a time. However, it helps to have at least one senior executive specifically assigned to the Marketing function. Preferably, they will, in turn, have at least two people designated to manage the two directions in the process, viz, "Promotion" and "Definition".

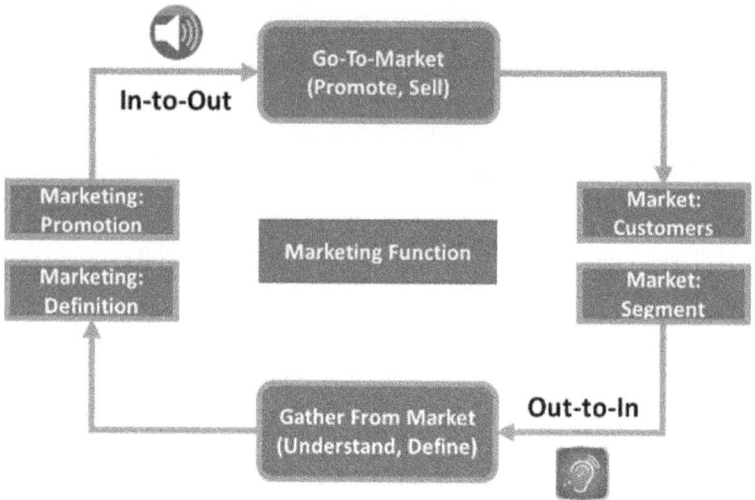

Fig. 3.2: Bi-Directional Marketing Function

Story of Ittiam's Commitment and Vision to Provide World-Class DSP Software

When Ittiam was founded by a team of experts in Digital Signal Processing (DSP) Software with proven experience working in Texas Instruments, the start-up's ability in the area was never questioned. The profound experience also allowed Ittiam to develop the initial suite of products based on an innate understanding of customer problems and market needs. However, Ittiam needed to invest much effort to keep this knowledge updated with the times, as shown in Fig 3.2. Ittiam's domain expertise meant customers could reduce their Time-To-Market (TTM) for their products and access field-proven intellectual property and technology.

The prospective customers welcomed the formation of such a company with a sharp focus on the field of mathematical and scientific specialization in Digital Signal Processing Software. Before the advent of Ittiam, the alternative independent source of DSP Software for the customers was possibly to engage in a development contract with a broad-based technology services company. However, the project would take much longer to realize and greater customer involvement to supervise the development. Further, the world-class performance of the software and proven reliability in the market were not guaranteed. Hence, some customers even appreciated us generously by saying, "I was looking for such a focused solution provider; where were you guys?".

The main question in the customers' minds was whether the start-up (Ittiam) would last for long and adopt a "customer-driven approach" to its operation.

The explicit communication of the customer problem-solving spirit, coupled with elucidating the start-up's dream and granting the stakeholder status to customer priorities, added immeasurable weight in convincing the customers to work with Ittiam.

Customer Acknowledgement Serves the Best Visibility

We discussed in the previous chapter that visibility is best created through third-party acknowledgments and neutral appreciation. The practical proof of this visibility in Ittiam's case was the public endorsements we could get from world-class customers when our products and solutions brought them significant measurable impact.

Customer endorsements manifested in many positive ways for Ittiam. They allowed Ittiam to showcase our technology with their products at specific world-class conferences in the common booth. Customers were generous to support a press release in which their head of research or marketing would provide a specific quote of value added by the Ittiam partnership.

Magazine articles highlighting the two companies' joint working added immense visibility.

Our investors used to appreciate such instances genuinely. In a lighter vein, they say that each such public mention is worth a hundred thousand dollars, roughly the amount we would otherwise have to spend in targeted advertisements to convey the same message.

Customer Visibility in the Era of Social Media

Ittiam's growth with products and customer endorsements in the 2000's happened in parallel with the growth of social media which has now become all encompassing. Some of the customer references were captured in the professional networking platform LinkedIn. A few of our product showcases were made available on YouTube. Such communications expanded the visibility in the new era of social media unfolding.

You can extend this concept to the present day to visualize the wonders your product breakthrough message with a leading customer acknowledgement can do in the social media post garnering tens of thousands of views and tens of prospective new customer leads coming back to you.

Building the Stakeholders' Spectrum

We can now build further the stakeholders' spectrum developed in the first two chapters with the top value creation areas for the customer.

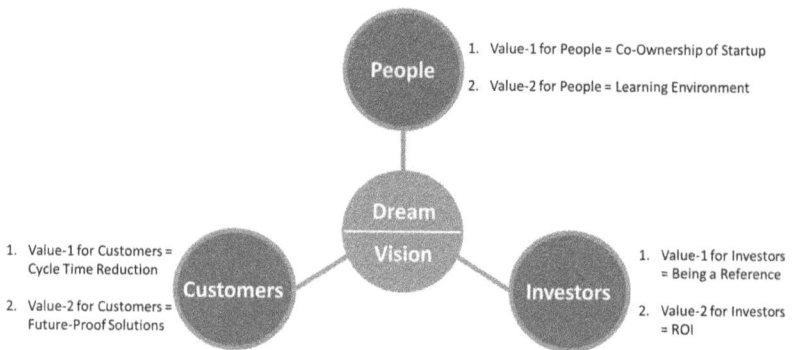

Fig. 3.3: Co-Owners of the Dream

Fig. 3.3 shows two top values that I recommend for consideration.

For example, if your start-up has the value proposition of saving precious time for the customer to go to market with their products and services, they will give you an audience to listen to you. That is a big first step achieved to take things forward. The second value proposition suggested is the essence of the problem-understanding and solving process shared in this chapter. It gives customers the confidence that they can depend on your solutions for the long term and that your support can be future-proof.

Treating this framework and suggestions as the starting point, you can think deeply and articulate your top values for the customers as you build out the stakeholders' spectrum.

Setting Up the Platforms for Stakeholders Interactions (PSI)

It is a privilege for a start-up to be blessed with the support of its own people, investors, and customers. Communication with them should not be just one-time or occasional but a continuous process. You should facilitate it by being right in the center of that communication network.

Amongst the three sets of stakeholders, the people (employees) of the start-up would have the most natural environment to interact among themselves frequently within the work environment. They will have opportunities to work, play and learn together daily.

Your start-up can require multiple investors. They could be a few or even several depending on the fundraising mode. It is common to have 2 or 3 investors at the beginning. New models are emerging where the funding comes in smaller quantities from each of several (tens of) investors, which, extended further, can become an extensive set of investors coming on board. Although multiple investors have invested in your start-up, you cannot expect them to have a natural inclination or time to come together to focus on your start-up's needs.

The stakeholders with the least interaction among them would be the customers. Firstly, they are all independent companies, potentially from different business segments, and even have a competitive charter between some of them. Each of them would require their business with the start-up to be strictly governed by confidentiality and Non-Disclosure Agreements (NDAs). The only way for them to meet up with others in the context of your start-up would be through a professional and safe platform to bring them with an objective, such as a product seminar or developers' workshop.

The start-up leadership must set up dedicated platforms for frequent interactions with each set of stakeholders. Exchange across the set is unlikely and may not be required. This Platform for Stakeholders Interaction (PSI) has immense benefits of having them all on the same page regarding start-up communications, listening to their unified voice, and generally boosting the morale and optimism of the start-up. These interaction mechanisms are listed here to get your creative thought process going and expand the mechanisms further.

People (Employees)

1. Monthly technical talks
2. Quarterly all-hands business updates
3. Annual day celebrations
4. Spontaneous team parties and picnics

Investors

1. Monthly reports
2. Quarterly board meetings
3. Offline updates and conference calls

Customers

1. Product seminars and showcases
2. Developers' workshop
3. Dinners and cocktails on the sidelines of major conferences

You and your leadership need to be the centre of gravity that pulls and anchors all these interactions. The interactions will not happen by themselves. It is in the start-up's best interest and squarely falls into its lap of responsibility.

All this could appear to be a lot of work, but it is both essential and worthwhile. When this platform and the interactions are shown pictorially, it will look like an impressive network, as shown in Fig. 3.4.

The forums shown in the network should run like well-oiled engines anchored by respective leaders in the start-up responsible for People, Investors, Customers and Overall. The exact CXO titles can vary from one start-up to another, but the responsibilities are well-mapped to the corresponding function in the start-up.

The Ship is Ready to Set Sail

The building of the ship is completed by bringing the customers on board. The Platform for Stakeholders Interaction sets the stage for continuous and harmonious communications from the start-up to all of them.

We are now ready to set sail and steer through the key challenges of the journey, beginning with the next part of three chapters.

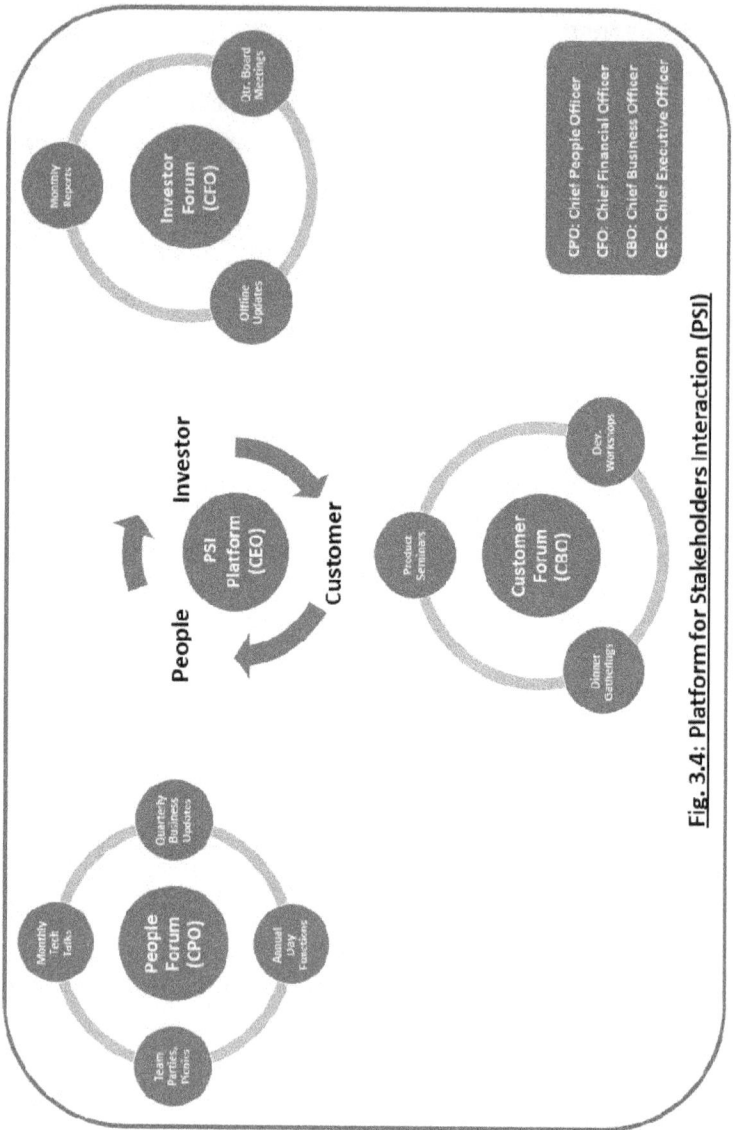

Fig. 3.4: Platform for Stakeholders Interaction (PSI)

Top Three Takeaways (T3)

1. Start-ups should appear to be anything but fly-by-night. Customers want a partner not only for today but for a long time. In turn, you want to win the customer for multiple instances of a business opportunity and life.

2. It is not only your technical competence but also the humility to understand customer problems and be a faithful servant all of which help start-ups win customers.

3. Have a dedicated process to guide and track customer problem-solving processes, as illustrated in Fig 3.1. That template is reproduced below with slight modifications for you to write down the notes with actual details of your start-up in each product or business segment you operate in.

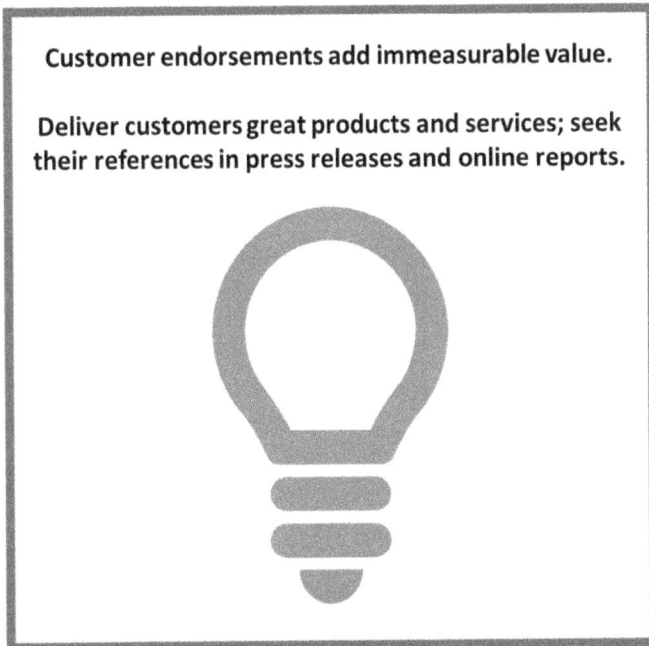

Customer endorsements add immeasurable value.

Deliver customers great products and services; seek their references in press releases and online reports.

A Light-Bulb Moment in Chapter-3

What is the important problem my customer faces?

How can I provide an efficient and unique solution?

Our Core Competencies

What needs to be done to make my customer succeed?

How can I help my customer verify that the solution works?

For Your T3 Notes from Chapter 3

4

Balancing Plan and Execution

Start-ups must achieve a fine balance between planning and execution. It is instinctive to jump into execution too soon. At the same time, a perfect plan can never be created without the lessons from execution.

Entrepreneurship is exciting because one can create something new that did not exist before. The entrepreneur starts with nothing. Well, almost nothing except their skills and confidence. The first asset they can create for the start-up is the "Plan", more commonly known as the "Business Plan."

The Business Plan is essential for everyone associated with the start-up, especially for the management, investors, product development, marketing, and sales teams. It states every important aspect of the start-up, including the following:

- Mission
- Market, customers, competitors
- Strategy and differentiation
- Product
- People

- Financials
- Risks
- Future roadmap

Planning is essential, but sometimes one can spend too much time on it. It is important to understand that there is only one way to be sure of how good the plan will be: when it is executed. Also, a business plan is like a brand-new car in the showroom – when it is written (driven out on the road), it becomes outdated. So, it needs to be kept continuously maintained and updated.

The Theme of Part II and Chapters 4 to 6

Before we delve into this chapter's focus on balancing plan and execution, it is helpful to note how the three chapters, 4, 5, and 6, will fit into the theme of Part II ("Steering").

Steering is about essential management decisions that need to be taken from time to time. Occasionally, the start-up can be in auto-pilot mode cruising on a straight line without any decision fork, but it would be a luxury more of an exception than the norm. The decisions arising can be day-to-day, periodic, sudden, or strategic. Through these three chapters, we will investigate three major balancing acts for decision-making in the start-up: Plan v Execution, Internal v External Funding, and Effort v Result.

These balancing decisions are merged into this middle part of the book since they are not standalone but linked to the overall goal of reaching home ("Shore" – Part III) while maximizing the structural assets of the start-up ("Ship" – Part I). In other words, they share a common theme and provide the perfect bridge in the middle to impact the elements in the preceding and succeeding parts.

To be complete, it must also be mentioned that a start-up would face other decisions to be made beyond the three key ones dealt with in this part. The methodology and rationale described in this part provide proper anchors to manage those decisions by preparing and acting on the required information with poise.

BALANCING PLAN AND EXECUTION

Planning and Execution in an Iterative Process

You can continuously improve the planning and execution through a well-structured and iterative process.

First things first, the business plan needs an owner. It's important to identify and assign an owner to the plan. There would be team members from different functions as required by the program who also need to be assigned.

The team led by the owner is responsible for creating the initial plan and reviewing it with management to align with the overall goals.

As the plan gets finalized, it must be supported with an execution engine that includes people, finances, facilities, and other resources.

The execution engine, a mechanism to track against the objectives, and further plan revisions to be completed during this process cycle are depicted in Fig. 4.1.

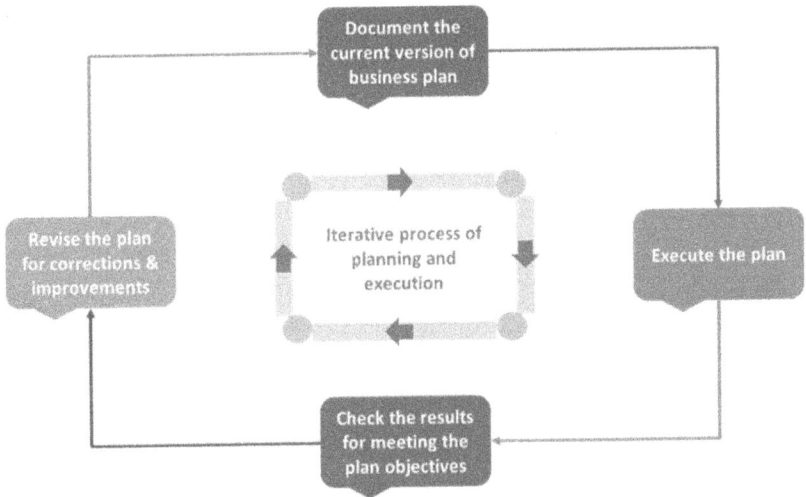

Fig. 4.1: Planning and Execution in Continuous Improvement Cycle

SRINI RAJAM

The Many Thrills of First Moments in Execution

Execution is when various people and teams involved in the plan experience the most incredible thrill and satisfaction. You want to record the precious moments in it for the archives. Here are a few of the iconic moments one looks forward to.

First Product Demo

All the hard work in product conception, design, debate, review, and development reaches fruition when the first demo works well at the touch of a keystroke or push of a button. There is genuine appreciation and uplifting of mood for everyone around. The technical team is elated, management confident, and the sales team is boosted to go on the roads. The demo could happen at an engineer's cubicle, lab, conference room, virtual meeting, or external event. Whatever the venue, it becomes the Olympic stadium for the product team to showcase their performance.

First Customer Win

A great product is a job well done, but it is only half the job. Ably supported by engineering and product teams, the marketing and sales teams are sweating it out to get that first customer win. The moment the customer says you are selected in a face-to-face meeting, sends the one-liner email, or drops a small purchase order for online signature, you know that your product is for real, and it has the first paying customer. Now, it promises to be the first of many more to come.

First Revenue Dollar

An anxious time gap exists between the first customer win and the first revenue dollar hitting your bank accounts. Many things taken for granted in the ordinary course of business must still happen correctly in this period. Your team must deliver the product package as agreed upon. The customer must receive, test, accept, and confirm it. Then, the invoice is raised, and payment is received. Of course, no unexpected cancellations should happen in this interim period. When the first payment is received, the team has an entirely different feeling. A start-up and business plan that is "revenue producing" has an altogether different body language and demeanor: optimistic, positive, and forward-looking.

First Break-Even and Profitable Year

One demo, win, and dollar do not make you profitable. The customer wins need to happen more and more. Profitability can be computed for different timeframes, one quarter, one year or over a cumulative period. For the first moment, anything will do. If you reckon the ship has sailed profitably for a month, quarter or year, then the know-how is in place to repeat the process, iron out the flaws and make it more sustainable. When the start-up operation turns profitable, it is one of the finest milestones in the journey. It is not only about that short period. It says a lot about the fundamental viability of the product and its value-addition to the customers. The practical results in the field have validated the theory in the business plan.

In the start-up world, the much-celebrated achievement is the *Break-Even Milestone*. It represents the year when the revenue from the business has met the entire operational expenses. Knowing that the start-up can pay for all its bills from customer payments is excellent. Things are getting in control. From here on, it is about growing the sales further, keeping the costs in proportion and extending the difference between the revenue and cost lines.

Two Old-School Virtues of All-Time Relevance

This is perhaps a good time to mention two old-school virtues that will always stand the start-up in good stead. The first is to hire people for the long term, and the second is to prioritise being profitable in a sustainable way and keep it going forever.

I am calling them old-school virtues since the emerging trends of some companies' cost reduction exercises include the undesirable practice of letting people go. On the second virtue, a few new business models prioritize on growth and other expansion metrics so much that having a fundamentally sound and profitable business operation takes a back seat.

On the first topic, we are all pragmatic to realize that people have all the freedom to change companies and careers to pursue the best path for themselves. The technology industry has been and will continue to manage significant employee turnover. While the freedom in that direction of decision-making, from employee to start-up, is fully understood, the point here is about the reverse direction. The people are part of the stakeholders' spectrum of the start-up. If the leadership has created a business plan that has failed, or the market assumptions have gone completely wrong, that is beyond what the people could have helped within their sphere of influence, and hence they cannot be held accountable. The talent coming into the start-up must be assessed and qualified for long-term retention. In addition to being the right thing to do, such a principle pays back in the form of universal respect and goodwill for the start-up in the professional community.

On keeping the top priority on being profitable, it is well understood that start-ups need a reasonable initial period to cross over the break-even point. After all, investing in deep technological capabilities, people resources, business channels, and infrastructure require a significant time and dollar investment. However, every effort must be made to retain that precious position when the first break-even or the steady state break-even is achieved after a couple of rounds of stabilization of the business cycle. This is a good practice advisory and a guideline that makes all the business sense. The power and flexibility that profitable state brings to the startup is immeasurable. For example, a prospective new investor discussion to drive growth can now be held from a position of strength. There is no unnecessary urgency to close the deal quickly since it is the money not needed to plug the leaking holes that could sink the boat but instead to find the next big sail to accelerate the journey. Many other important decisions, such as bringing in top talent and rewarding the high-performance teams to differentiate in the market, are all within the management's control when the ship is sailing profitably. As one of our investors used to put it succinctly, *when you are profitable, you control your destiny.*

The last important point of this section is that you can still achieve good growth while prioritizing profitability. For example, strong profits and financial reserves enable a start-up to respond quickly to new business opportunities. It can mobilize all the development, marketing and sales resources needed to realize the opportunity, at least partially even if not fully. With the strength of such a foundation established, additional external capital can be raised faster and on better terms if required. Cycle time for decision making and execution is perhaps the most important factor in driving growth. The profitable state correlates superbly with speed of action. In our experience in Ittiam, there are several instances of addressing expansion opportunities expeditiously through internal reserves built over years of sustained profitability.

Retaining Business Plan Relevance to Start-up Objectives

Let us turn our attention from the landmarks and excitement of execution towards the big picture.

The business plan must always remain relevant to the start-up's overall objectives.

As you go deep into the execution phase and work through its challenges, the big picture can sometimes be lost, thus creating a disconnect with the overall objectives. For example, should there be key changes in the environment that impact the objectives and assumptions, the plan must change as well. This directly relates to the revision step captured in Fig. 4.1.

The point about retaining relevance can be highlighted with a hypothetical example.

Consider the early 2000s when digital cameras were produced and sold as a standalone product rather than integrated into smartphones. At that time, it was perfectly understandable for a start-up to have a 3-

year business plan to design, produce and sell a certain number of digital cameras and capture a target percentage of market share for that product within a given market region.

The management could have signed off on this plan, and the project kicked off and progressed, tracked every quarter over 12 quarters making up the three years. After a year into this plan, if the start-up realized that camera features integrated into phones were coming up thick and fast in the market trend and would soon become the way of life for consumers, would it make sense to continue rigorously executing and track the original plan? No. The market dynamics would call for a complete recalibration of product strategy and business plan.

This is the kind of market awareness and agility that a start-up must exhibit and adapt to the planning and execution steps of the business process.

Recall from Chapter 2, when discussing the key factors in investor assessment, the common philosophy in the investment fraternity is to *"bet on people rather than one particular idea."* You can now see how appropriate that is in the context of retaining relevance and the example reviewed here. If the business plan signed off by the investor was the brightest idea at that time, but the team needed to be more resourceful, their chances of successfully adapting to the market dynamics would not be good. However, if the investors bet on an A-Team, even if the first idea (business plan) conceived was not the greatest, the team is most likely to learn, adapt and succeed within the normal time.

Framework to Connect from Dream to Plan

Considering the business plan relevance and continuous alignment discussed so far, you would be well-served by creating a top-down chart, beginning from the start-up's Dream to Vision and Mission, Strategic Objectives and Business Plan as depicted in Fig. 4.2.

This illustration chart in Fig. 4.2 is for a hypothetical start-up with a Business Plan to build a Smartphone App Software for advanced camera function and sell it on the Android and iOS App Stores. Let us say it is the same team from the previous case, which started with the right idea at that time for making and selling standalone digital cameras but quickly realized that the same capability delivered as a Smartphone App would make a better business case in the emerging times. So, the investors had bet on a competent team.

You first notice that the chart presents the instant link to all the activities and decisions, from the big picture to detailed actions.

The important characteristic of this top-down link is that as you traverse the chart from top to bottom, the frequency at which an element in the chart can change increases.

Illustrative Tops Down Chart

Illustrative Tops Down Chart

Statement of Dream (Passion) – Applicable for the Long Term
To be filled up

Statement of Vision – Applicable Over ~5 Years
To be filled up

Statement of Mission – Applicable Over ~3 Years
To be filled up

Strategic Objective #1	Strategic Objective #2	Strategic Objective #3
To be filled up	To be filled up	To be filled up

Business Plan in Support of Above Framework (Plans for Multiple Distinct Businesses Can be Prepared Separately and Consolidated for Overall Plan)

Business Plan Data	Year-1	Year-2	Year-3	Remarks
Total Available Market (TAM)	1,000,000	1,200,000	1,500,000	Total Available Opportunity for the Business
No. of Software (App) Units Sold	10,000	50,000	100,000	Indicates Market Share and Growth Potential
Unit Price of Software	2.50	3.00	3.50	Defines the Basic Market Value of Product
Total Revenue	25,000	150,000	350,000	(No. of Units Sold) x (Unit Price)
Number of People	20	25	30	Factor of Direct Expenses
Total Cost (People, Direct and Indirect)	100,000	130,000	150,000	Includes All Expenses
Gross Profit (EBITDA)	(75,000)	20,000	200,000	Profit Before All Deductions
Cumulative Gross Profit / Loss	(75,000)	(55,000)	145,000	Cumulative Break-Even Reached in Year-3

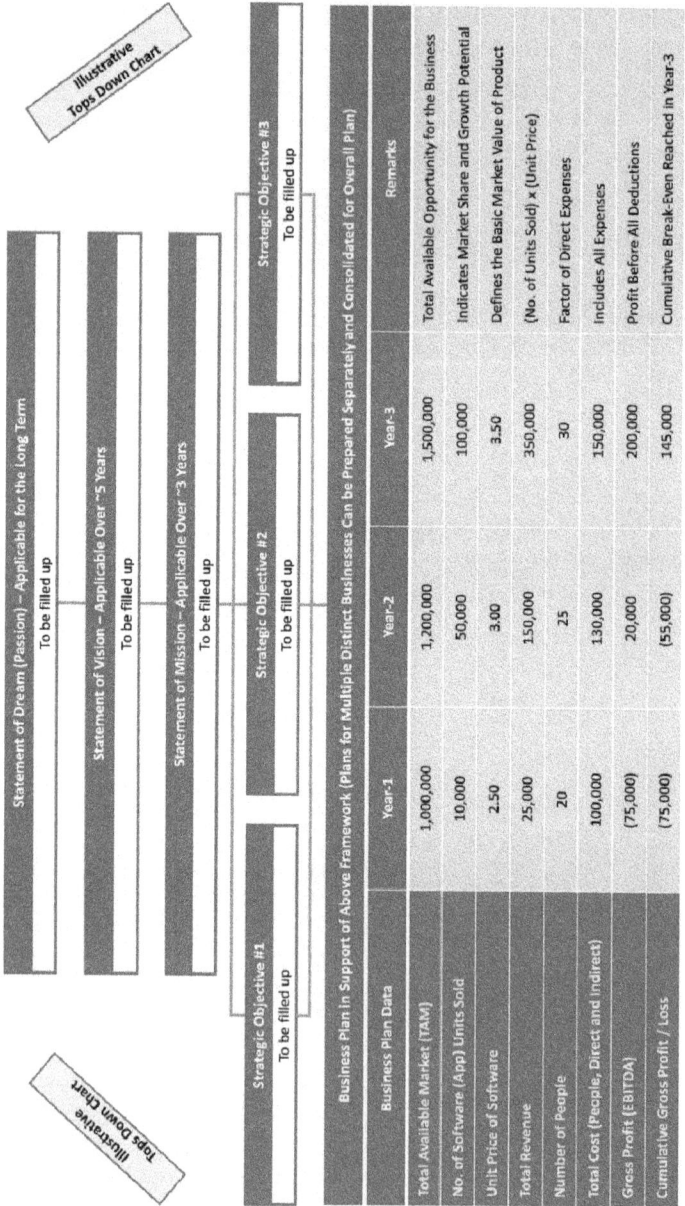

Fig. 4.2: Tops Down Framework to Connect from Dream to Plan

The Dream should hardly change, and the vision can transform once in several years. Still, in the end, the Business Plan must be quite agile and respond dynamically, say, half-yearly or even quarterly.

You can view this chart as a starting template. You can upgrade it for your specific situation and populate the various sections with actual information which will be proprietary and confidential to your start-up.

Top Three Takeaways (T3)

1. A business plan is essential, but it is not cast in concrete. Start-ups must be flexible to modify the plan based on learnings from execution and dynamic changes in the market environment.

2. Execution must start early, and continuous adaptation is a must. It is better to fail fast than to go down extremely slowly, resulting in a much more significant loss for the start-up. Planning and execution can go hand in hand to create a continuously tracking and improving process.

3. The business plan needs to link up to the start-up dream and vision. As proposed in Fig. 4.2, the framework helps achieve that. A generic and unfilled version is given below for your notes from this chapter.

Business Plan is the reference which guides all the internal functions and investor discussions.

Execution helps the Plan to evolve and be relevant.

A Light-Bulb Moment in Chapter-4

BALANCING PLAN AND EXECUTION

Statement of Dream (Passion) – Applicable for the Long Term
To be filled up

Statement of Vision – Applicable Over ~5 Years
To be filled up

Statement of Mission – Applicable Over ~3 Years
To be filled up

Strategic Objective #1
To be filled up

Strategic Objective #2
To be filled up

Strategic Objective #3
To be filled up

Generic Template to Link from Dream to Plan

Business Plan in Support of Above Framework (Plans for Multiple Distinct Businesses Can be Prepared Separately and Consolidated for Overall Plan)

Business Plan Data	Year-1	Year-2	Year-3	Remarks
Total Available Market (TAM)				Total Available Opportunity for the Business
No. of Product Units Sold				Indicates Market Share and Growth Potential
Unit Price of Product				Defines the Basic Market Value of Product
Total Revenue				(No. of Units Sold) x (Unit Price)
Number of People				Factor of Direct Expenses
Total Cost (People, Direct and indirect)				Includes All Expenses
Gross Profit (EBITDA)				Profit Before All Deductions
Cumulative Gross Profit / Loss				Cumulative Break-Even Reached in Year-3

For Your T3 Notes from Chapter 4

5

Balancing Internal Funding and External Venture Capital

It is better to have an idea that requires money to succeed than a lot of money staying idle for an idea to germinate. Timing and type of external capital partnerships are among entrepreneurs' most critical decisions.

Everything a start-up does must be relevant and aligned to reaching home and steering the ship to the shore. We already noted in the introduction of the previous chapter that the three Chapters, 4 to 6, comprising Part II, fit into the theme of key decisions and balancing acts that the start-up leadership must perform towards the overall goal ("Shore") through maximal leverage of the available assets ("Ship")

If one decision is more relevant to the outcome described above than most other elements, it would be the nature and scope of external funding raised by the start-up. Why? This is because the investors have a significant say not only in where the start-up can reach but also in how the start-up can navigate towards that.

The start-up may seek finances ("Debt") from external sources such as banks and financial institutions to run its business. A simple and common form of financing is through loans with the associated repayment terms and period. The interest rates and regular repayment schedules are typically not easily affordable by a start-up since it needs to invest upfront to create its products and establish its business. In its early stages, the start-up's revenue and cash flow are not predictable enough to work off a standard loan. "Venture Capital" offers an excellent alternative for start-up financing since the venture capital institutions are designed to take higher risk for higher returns. For example, they can fund a start-up in return for taking a certain percentage of equity ownership in the start-up.

While it may not be apparent, venture capital is said to be the most expensive form of debt. The return payment is made through company shareholding and certain investor rights. In the long run, when the company is performing well, these will be of much greater value going out of the company than servicing a loan on fixed terms. For example, the company would pay dividends from profits and the share price grows in value based on company performance. On the other hand, if the company is not doing well, the rights given to the investor could lead to heavy payments back to them depending on the conditions agreed upon in the investment shareholding agreement.

Despite the pros and cons of venture capital briefly stated above, the venture capital investor is considered the start-up's preferred type of financial partner in the industry. Hence significant executive time and effort from the start-up are required to fully understand and set up the partnership for mutual success.

Of course, as part of building the start-up ship, we treat the investor as vital and integral part of the stakeholders' spectrum. In line with the approach presented in Chapter 2 to select the investors carefully, at any given instance, balancing the external capital to be raised with internal funds available is also a conscious exercise to be undertaken.

Do Start-ups Have the Luxury of Internal Funds and Balancing?

The first question arising in our minds could be whether start-ups would have sufficient internal funds to utilize and balance against other external sources. Are they not supposed to be requiring venture capital by definition? This may not always be the case, and there are a few precious sources of internal funding to consider.

The founding team members bring in some initial, albeit modest, funds to set up the starting capital base. Thus, the start-up has some working capital to begin with. During the journey, the start-up will have revenue accruals from selling products and services to customers, which is an important reserve to consider. In certain exceptional situations, where the start-up has cutting-edge technology and development in the works, a customer might be willing to engage in a "paid program" that gives them early access to the technology. This could serve as partial funding for the start-up.

External investment requirements particularly arise initially and after a few years when new product ideas and potentially orbit-changing opportunities arise. Start-ups launching a completely new strategic direction are set to be "pivoting", and extensive new capital infusion by investors usually accompanies that. In the later stages of the journey, if the start-up has crossed the important break-even milestone in its operations, it would have some internal cash reserves from its profits.

Let us consider a start-up in mid-course planning for an expansion and able to finance itself through internal resources and customer revenues. The fact that it is preparing for expansion and does not require external capital would be a very strong statement. Ironically, it may attract many investment proposals even though it is not looking for investment. However, such a case would be more of an exception than the norm. Not all start-ups would be in such a position, especially in the early stages. Many examples of external capital provide growth impetus and strategic advantage to a start-up. In Ittiam's case, after we reached the first instance of solid profitability in the fourth year, the second round of investment from a major global investor helped the company to accelerate new product lines and international market expansion. Growth-oriented investments typically aim to strengthen the start-up's R&D capacity, industry partnerships and global footprint. Two important decisions to be made in the investment situation are 1) the Quantum of external capital to be raised and 2)

Identifying the right investor source and convincing them to be a part of the dream and journey.

One thumb rule is to raise external capital no more than the operating budget needed for one year or 18 months at the outer limit. This assumes that the start-up would be running well enough to be self-sufficient from the second year or latest, after a year and a half. This approach will be especially suitable for services and solutions-oriented business models.

We will look at a slightly more refined approach below for product-oriented start-ups.

Cash Flow and Minimum Viable Product (MVP) Model for Capital Requirement

If your start-up business strategy is built around a key product, the cash flow analysis for getting to the Minimum Viable Product (MVP) stage is a logical approach to determine the external capital requirement.

In general, for product-oriented start-ups, investors' confidence will increase by leaps and bounds when they can touch and feel something. A demonstrable initial product is significantly more credible than many product presentations and specification documents. Accordingly, the valuation investors are willing to assign to the start-up also improves.

At the MVP stage, you have developed the product with sufficient basic features to demonstrate to potential customers and partners. You showcase what the product is all about even though the MVP version is still being prepared for production release to the broad market. An early-adopter customer can use the product to check it out and give valuable feedback. This has the twin benefits of developing the interest of the future customer and guiding the product development team with more precise requirements for further development. The MVP also helps validate major product plan assumptions and identify potential roadblocks early in the process.

From the above, we can realize that reaching the MVP stage overall impacts positively on the start-up's investors, customers, and internal teams.

Typical MVP development cycle time would be short, about 6-9 months. The team strength required to accomplish this depends on the product's complexity and the teams tend to be lean. The focus is on agile development.

Linking this back to external funding requirements, it would be quite a logical step if you set the external capital size equal to the finance necessary to get to the MVP stage. This involves higher risk than raising capital for a 12–18-month window but has the potential reward that you can get greater investor interest and better valuation prospects at the MVP stage.

Basic Valuation Framework

Understanding the basic principles of valuation is essential so that you are entirely in tune with how the mechanism works.

We often hear investors saying they are always willing to invest in a good company IF the valuation is right. That is indeed a big if. Hearing such a statement gives an initial feeling that you have a great opportunity with them, but it may be more complex. What does it mean? It means that they want to avoid overpaying for the share, and the quality of the start-up from an investor perspective is not a standalone factor but is always seen in conjunction with its price or valuation.

Let us view this Quality-Price duo from two ends of the valuation spectrum.

If a start-up were theoretically valued at zero, the investor would not hesitate to invest since the entire company can be taken over for nothing. Extending this further, if you were willing to offer the shares at an attractive price, implying some undervaluing of the start-up, there is an excellent chance of closing the deal. All this is still under the assumption that the start-up passes the primary quality gate with flying colors.

At the other end of the spectrum, even if they come across the best-in-class start-up, but its share value has already shot up to an astronomical price, the investors would be wary of investing in it. This indicates that the start-up's current high valuation can sometimes deter attracting certain types of investors, even though they may be most desirable to partner with considering all other factors. We will come to this aspect again soon.

Remember, from an investor's perspective, the future is more important than the past as far as price and valuation are concerned. This means they want to invest at a price where the start-up has immense potential to grow its performance and accordingly, multiply the share price.

The graphic below in Fig. 5.1 illustrates the basic equation for raising capital. Simply put, the current valuation of the start-up plus the capital raised becomes the future valuation of the start-up, post the investment transaction. One of the critical takeaways evident from the graphic is that raising capital way above the start-up's current valuation (called "pre-money valuation" in investment terminology) is not advisable since it reduces the start-up's shareholding percentage and company control significantly. As a simple case of the equation, if the start-up raises additional capital equal to its current valuation, its shareholding after the investment round comes down to 50%.

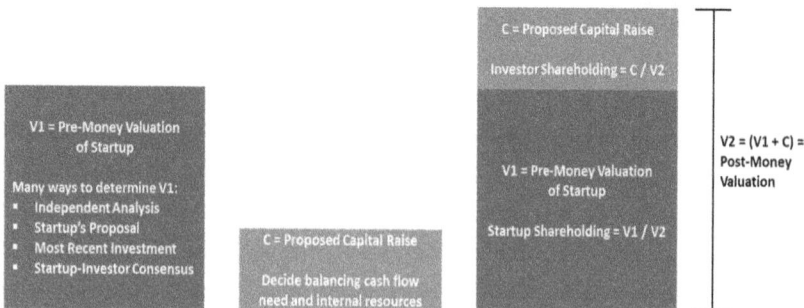

Fig. 5.1: Basic Valuation Framework

Setting the Pre-Money Valuation

From the basic valuation framework of Fig. 5.1, the key unknown and intriguing question is, how is the pre-money valuation determined? Different financial methods are available to determine a company's value and independent valuation agencies could be employed to provide a certified opinion. Ultimately, this is a number that the start-up and investor must agree upon. Their proposal will have a greater say depending on who is stronger at the discussion table. From the start-up's perspective, proposing the appropriate valuation to the investor requires balancing two opposing considerations described here.

It is in the start-up's best interest to analyze from the investor's perspective and propose for pre-money valuation to proactively steer the discussions toward convergence. Starting at an unrealistically high valuation can put off investor interest in beginning the dialog. The initially proposed valuation should not be too low either since it would only go in one direction during the discussions, i.e., downwards, reducing the start-up's shareholding percentage. It is a delicate balance. It helps to be realistic, do the homework, and convey that you are fully aware of the conditions.

Investors typically consider the following factors in determining the pre-money valuation:

1. Valuation metric used in the previous round of investment, if applicable

2. Current year revenue and 3-year projection, if a start-up has already reached the revenue stage

3. Current year profit and 3-year projection, if a start-up has already reached profitability

4. Intellectual property held by the start-up

5. Valuation of comparator companies

6. Cash reserves in the start-up

Given your industry, established valuation metrics are linked to the factors [1] through [6]. For example, hi-tech industries get a higher multiple of their revenue and profit number as valuation compared to the multiples for very mature industries.

An indicative and generic formula for valuation can be expressed in the following manner.

$$V = C + (m1 * R)$$
$$V = C + (m2 * P)$$

V: Valuation	C: Cash Reserves
R: Revenue	m1: Revenue Multiplier
P: Profit	m2: Profit Multiplier

C is the free cash reserves in the start-up. The profit multiplier m2 is a larger number than the revenue multiplier m1, because that profit is a smaller percentage of the revenue. To understand m2 for different industry segments, one can study the publicly available stock market data and look at the P/E Ratio (Price to Earnings Ratio). Earnings here refer to the company's "Earnings Per Share". P/E Ratio shows what the market is willing to pay today for a stock based on its earnings. In principle, for a start-up, m2 is the equivalent of P/E for listed companies in that industry segment. As mentioned, the hi-tech industry commands a higher P/E ratio of 10 and up to 25. More established and mature industries get a lower P/E. P/E ratio is a reflection of the market's confidence in the prospects of the industry in general and the company in particular.

Regarding its sensitivity to the valuation of start-ups, the most interesting of the factors above is 'C,' or cash reserves. When that number is substantial, it has a moderate, additive influence on the valuation. However, it can have a huge negative impact when it gets dangerously low and close to zero. That scenario means you are running out of cash and risk the continuity of the start-up. There is extreme pressure to close a new investment quickly. The higher the vulnerability, the lower the valuation drives towards, even if the start-up is making decent revenue and profit.

Specials Cases of Setting Pre-Money Valuation

We noted in the previous section that the valuation metric used in the prior investment round plays a role in setting a pre-money valuation for the next round.

Should a start-up always look to raise capital at a pre-money valuation equal to or greater than the previous round? In general, this is a good and expected practice since it protects the investments made by everyone so far into the company. If you were an investor who bought a start-up's shares at a price equal to X, you would not like to see the start-up issuing fresh shares to the next investor at a price discounted over X.

However, there can be valid exceptions. Here are descriptions of two such cases, one of strategic nature and the other representing a somewhat tricky situation.

At the growth inflection stage of a start-up, the key to success may lie with a strategic customer partner who can potentially open large markets and lay the platform to rapidly expand the start-up business. They may require making an equity investment and influencing the company's direction to strengthen the relationship. Further, in their independent assessment, they may determine and propose making that investment at a nominal discount over the previous round. Should the start-up walk away from such an orbit-changing opportunity over the issue of the proposed valuation being slightly lower than the last round?

This investment proposal could be extremely important to the start-up, its management, and all the investors already on board, and it requires a dedicated open discussion among the stakeholders. A natural consensus that we can expect to be reached is that all the present stakeholders welcome the new investor for the greater good and accept the nominal impact on the valuation.

Further, the process can become more amenable for everyone by opening the new investment round (at a lower price) to all the current stakeholders. Not all may want to participate, but it is an important step in the fairness process that they all have been given the option. Those who choose to participate benefit from averaging their investment price in the start-up over the two rounds. Hence, this could turn into an optimistic and welcoming scenario overall.

The second case is a difficult one. It is common for a start-up valuation to come down due to poor performance, emerging unfavorable market conditions, or results not in line with the aggressive projections made earlier, based on which the earlier valuation could have been set. All the investors currently on board would hope for the issues to be resolved quickly with strong improvements shown by the start-up. However, if new capital raise is a must for the start-up to sustain the operation or fund a new initiative, everyone would need to reach a pragmatic conclusion that the new investment must happen at a lower valuation than the previous round. Existing investors may make this investment so that the story "remains within." However, there have also been cases where a new investor comes on board at a lower valuation, with some existing investors also participating in the latest round. The modalities of the two cases discussed here look similar. Still, the investment motivations are contrasting, one driven by strategic potential and the other by the critical issues prevailing in the start-up.

Start-up vs. Investor is NOT a David vs. Goliath Story

Are the investors too powerful and the start-up the underdog?

A small start-up raising capital from a prominent investor should not be seen as David vs. Goliath match-up, even though it may be fascinating to visualize it in that manner. The rationale for this comes from the fact that it is unclear who is David and who is Goliath, as both parties are taking on high odds. Both are fighting to win in a very uncertain situation.

Looking from the venture capital investor lens, the capital invested is, after all, totally unsecured. The bottom line is that there is no fixed asset or collateral to recover the investment should the start-up fail or perform below expectations to provide meaningful returns. Hence from the investor perspective, they are taking a huge risk.

Likewise, from the start-up lens, the repayment terms for the capital received are not fixed like a standard loan from a bank. Typically, the capital stays in the form of equity shares and company shareholding allocated to the investor. In other words, "they become a part of the company." Should the start-up grow 10X in value, so does the investor's return, and should it shrink 10X in value, so does the return.

Further, the investor can hold certain special rights, such as exercising veto in decision-making; they can ask for their shareholding percentage not to be reduced ("diluted") in subsequent rounds of investment; they can and will control the start-up's direction. So, from the start-up perspective too, a huge commitment and risk are being made.

In the final analysis, we must remember that external investors and investments bring credibility and stability to the start-up. Still, the capital does come at a cost that needs to be well understood.

A lasting takeaway from this discussion could be that you do not want to raise capital more than the minimum level necessary. Of course, in an economic downturn, one tends to raise more than necessary, and vice versa in an economic boom. The market jargon in an economic recession is *Cash is the King*. You want to secure the maximum reserves for the start-up to last the distance. The jargon in the boom times is that *Paper is the King*. You are willing to wait to maximize the value of your paper (share certificate) when the investment climate peaks to its best.

Useful Reference from Ittiam Experience

From my Ittiam experience, we will add useful references to this chapter's focus on balancing internal funding with external venture capital.

To highlight how selective and careful we have been in raising external capital, we have had only two external investments in the first two decades of our operation from 2001-20. The first was from Global Technology Ventures (GTV), which became a part of Coffee Day Enterprises. The second was from Bank of America Equity Partners, which later became the fund known as NewQuest Capital Partners.

During these 20 years, many new experiments and ventures including our foray into Computer Vision and Retail Visual Analytics were funded exclusively from the internal reserves of Ittiam. Managing the start-up consistently profitably and financially prudently provided us with invaluable freedom and flexibility to carry out the new experiments on our own accord.

Finally in 2021, to sharpen our technological and strategic direction, Ittiam raised investment from Dolby Laboratories, a world-renowned leader in audio and media technologies.

Of course, as emphasized throughout the book, all the investors have been integral to the company and a key part of our stakeholders' spectrum.

Where Are We Now

We are in the phase of the start-up journey, steering the ship, where the Plan and Execution modes are dynamically balanced, and the Internal and External funding sources are also optimally aligned.

The next critical tool in the steering phase is how we manage ourselves daily. Rome was not built in a day. At the same time, you also want to know at the end of every day, week, or month that the efforts are producing the results as intended. The next chapter leads us to this important balancing act between actions and results.

Top Three Takeaways (T3)

1. In the final analysis, external investment is part and parcel of start-up life. It's worth remembering that external investors and investment bring credibility and stability to the start-up, but the capital does come at a cost that needs to be well understood.

2. Prepare a 2-year cash flow worksheet for your business plan without using external capital as a starting point. From there, determine the range (Min - Nom - Max) within which external capital is required and how it will affect the shareholding table. For example, for a product start-up, you can use the MVP model discussed earlier to set the Min. Nom would be slightly more conservative to secure funding for 12 months to cover the operational expenses. At the Max number, you would look at 18-24 months for operational stability and weathering any macroeconomic storms on the horizon.

3. You are now poised to prepare a shortlist of potential investor sources to be approached, their merits and demerits in the context of the company's Purpose-Vision-Strategy, and finally, the preferred order in which the list of investor sources would be approached for investment dialogue. Chapter 2 has provided a good background for engaging with prospective investors in a two-way dialogue and bringing on board the one(s) who will enhance the stakeholders' spectrum of your start-up.

Even if the business is healthy in Profit & Loss (P&L) terms, thin cash reserves puts everyone on the edge.

Good reserves give you stability and assure continuity.

A Light-Bulb Moment in Chapter-5

6

Balancing Process Efforts and Result Orientation

A start-up achieves world-class results through the best-in-class efforts that it puts in. Too much obsession with the results can sometimes distract the start-up from focusing on those efforts. Conversely, treating the efforts as an end goal leads to missing the big picture. Efforts and Results must be in balance. It helps to have a little bias towards efforts to lessen the pressure and allow the important activities to proceed normally.

Cricket, played globally since the 19th century, is incredibly influential in India and a way of life for the people of India. Cricket gets the high mindshare of sporting life in many other countries, including Australia, Bangladesh, England, New Zealand, Pakistan, South Africa, Sri Lanka, and The West Indies (Caribbean Islands). Cricket intrinsically creates massive data of individual performances, team scores, results, and records. The game is called a *statistician's delight*, but the data deluge can sometimes distract the players' focus.

Its purest form is called Test Cricket which is played over five days. That format tests sustained excellence over long periods, strategy, and perseverance. In its shortest forms of 50-overs and 20-overs, the matches conclude in 8 and 4 hours, respectively. These versions are incredibly focused on instant results and gratification. In those formats, the captain who is regarded as the most astute and successful is India's M S Dhoni (fondly called MSD by his fans). He has won three global titles for India, in World Cups and Champions Trophy, in addition to numerous wins in Franchise Leagues and Tournaments. This is more than any other captain has ever won or what most captains can even dream of.

At major post-match conferences and triumphant occasions, when asked about the secret of success for him and his team, MSD typically has one answer: "We focus on doing the fundamental processes well, and the result takes care of itself." This incredible belief, commitment, and statement comes from *Captain Extraordinaire* in a world where everyone craves immediate results and is anxious about what will happen next. Is it possible to calm one's mind so beautifully to keep doing the right things repeatedly and not fret over the outcome?

The start-up's and its people's mind is similar to the sporting situation described above. Every day, the mind wanders from doing things to looking over the results and coming back to doing things. People are coached, managed, and reviewed for following world-class processes as well as achieving world-beating results. Their mind is restless.

When you are in the thick of the action with the start-up journey, this single area can make a big difference in the type of team you would create. Turn the knob slightly towards the efforts and continue doing things well; you could have a group enjoying, performing, focused, and succeeding. Turn the knob intensely toward results, and your team could be on the other side of the fence, anxious, running around crazily, distracted, and living on the edge for the results.

Of course, we all know that the winner takes it all, and we do not want to end up as the honorable second. But what mindset does it take to be a winner in the first place?

Story from the World of Snooker

"Success vs. Joy" is a book by Geet Sethi, a seven times world billiards champion, where he presents his experiences about sharing joy and what society views as success. His succinctly powerful line says, "Joy is internal – Success is a creation of society." Perhaps a lesson for the start-up teams is to be in it for the love and joy of doing what they do best.

One of the illustrations in Chapter XII of that book *("Snatching Defeat from the Jaws of Victory")* talks about a young snooker player from Thailand (a country not so well known for Snooker), James Wattana. In 1989 when he was only 18, Wattana was taking on the celebrated British Champion, Jimmy White, in the semi-finals of Mita World Masters, "a snooker tournament in which the first prize was a towering 200,000 British Pounds (at that time, it was the biggest winner's cheque in the game's history)".

Wattana was going well against White, leading 8-6 in a best-of-19-frames match. A momentary distraction from Wattana thinking about what he can do with the winning prize money rather than focusing on the job at hand made him miss a straightforward pivotal pot. He went on to lose the match 8-10. When Wattana missed that simple pot, even the audience at the National Exhibition Center in Birmingham was stunned.

As the book captures vividly, a reporter in the pressroom after the match asked Wattana why he had lost even after being in the lead. He replied with remarkable candor, "When I led 8-6, my mind wandered to this specific street in Bangkok where there is a house that I wanted to buy for my mother with the prize money." Wattana's concentration was lost due to a possibility in the future, and he could never fully focus back to the effort required to accomplish the desired result in the present.

This touching story highlights the importance of focusing, keeping the mind calm about the result, and concentrating on what needs to be done.

Results and Visibility Snowball in a Start-up

Naturally, significant results get greater visibility in a start-up where every day counts, and you are trying to make tangible progress in every step.

Like the thrill moments we touched upon during the execution phase in Chapter 4, a world-class product performance, a significant customer win, and a milestone revenue attainment are results that get excellent visibility, and that combination has a snowballing effect. Celebration of such successful milestones is essential to sustaining positivity in the start-up world where things are always up and down, and a crisis can pop up anytime.

However, to ensure that all the above is achievable, startups must keep certain fundamental activities running at the same level or even higher efficiency, enthusiasm and accuracy. For example, despite product release pressures, the team must maintain adequate focus on the design review step, system test, and quality control check post. Products released in haste make it impossible to scale up to future demands. The bigger problem is waiting to strike soon. We can easily visualize how similar situations in other areas, such as talent training and development, business development programs, and long-term infrastructure set-up, must function efficiently and maturely.

We want to showcase and reward outstanding results while recognizing and strengthening the underlying mechanisms that produce those results.

Organisational Framework to Review Progress on Process and Result Dimensions

How does a start-up organization function and deliver? From a layperson's point of view, several people may appear to be busy doing many things in their ways. Still, producing the results takes a well-defined set of methods or processes that bring together the people and their activities.

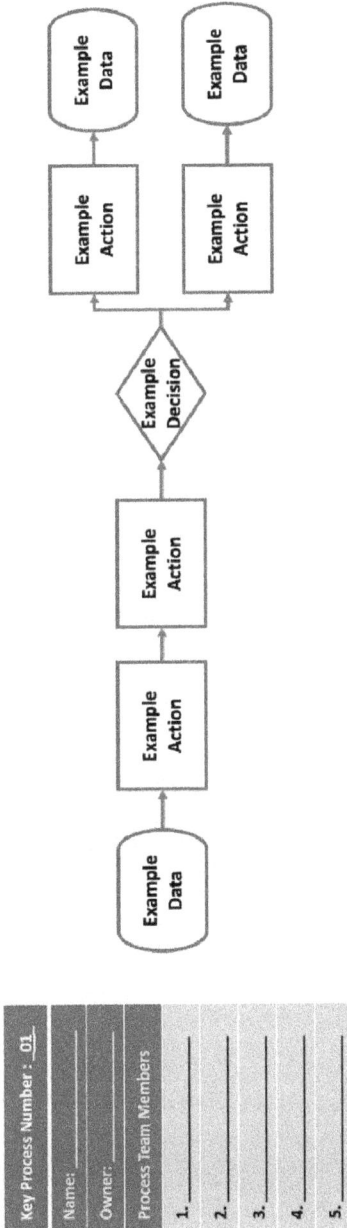

Fig. 6.1: Process Documentation Example

Organizations function through a well-defined set of processes. For example, hiring new talent for the start-up is a process. It can embed within itself sub-processes such as, in this case, the written test process, interview process, and employment offer process. Similarly, many things we take for granted intuitively have underlying processes. They include areas critical for the start-up, such as product marketing (refer to Chapter 3 on customer problem understanding), new customer development, sales proposal, and customer support.

It is important to document each essential process. The illustrative template in Fig. 6.1 can be a starting point for further adaptation. It defines the process owner and team members. It describes the key actions and decisions involved in the process and the relevant data repository updated. The activities captured can be self-contained or can, in turn, invoke another process which would be termed as a "sub-process" to this "parent process."

In line with the focus of this chapter, let us consider the combined picture of key processes along with the key result areas.

While the Key Result Areas (KRAs) instantly get the mindshare of everyone in the start-up, we want the Key Processes underlying the success of the Key Result Areas to be on the same page. Hence, the next useful documentation is creating the map between those two dimensions, as illustrated in Fig. 6.2.

Such a map instantly highlights the impact of each key process on the various results. Alternatively, it also captures for each result the processes it depends on.

Map of Key Result Area (KRA) / Key Process	KRA-1	KRA-2	...	KRA-(n-1)	KRA-n
Key Process 1	★			★	★
Key Process 2		★		★	
...					
Key Process (n-1)					★
Key Process n	★				

Fig. 6.2: Map of Key Result Area – Key Process

These two documents lay the foundation for creating a balanced mix of process-oriented and result-oriented review frameworks for teams and individuals. You are sending a positive message to everyone on the team that they must excel in both dimensions. The team members will also be clear and happy that their contributions on both dimensions are being recognized and rewarded.

The performance review table in Fig. 6.3 presents a suggestive framework. A healthy mix of entries in column "Type" will ensure that excellence in process and result are comprehended.

Illustrative Performance Review Framework for Teams and Individuals					
Performance Description	Type	Goal Set	Attainment	Reward	Remarks
	Process Adoption				
	Process Compliance				
	Process Innovation				
	Business Target				
	People Target				
	Customer Target				

Fig. 6.3: Balanced Mix of Process and Result Metrics

Process Compliance Requirements, Customer Collaboration, and Co-Creation

In addition to driving quality and efficiency, process focus positively impacts working with major customers and strategic partners.

Firstly, depending on the start-up's industry and domain, successful compliance and certification to certain process standards would be mandatory to work with customers. They are likely to thoroughly review the start-up's processes or study its latest certification results to be sure that it can be depended upon for sustained excellence and output. General industry certifications such as ISO9000 have been practiced for a long time. The process requirements can be highly specialized to the specific domains of the start-up. For example, software standards compliance is the field of specialization to make software safe and secure for users. They can cover the entire gamut of software development and deployment.

Beyond standards compliance, some customers may present the start-up with unique opportunities for advanced technology, product co-creation, and joint intellectual property filings at higher levels of collaboration. Participating in such projects will require the start-up's processes to be transparent and compatible with the customer's processes. For example, suppose your new product development methodology has a set of well-defined steps, 1 through n, for co-creation. In that case, the customer's R&D effort may enter at step 3 in your process and exit together at step-n or in some other such configuration.

Process compatibility with customers is almost taken for granted in well-established activities such as customer support and financial systems. In many industries, customer problem logs and resolutions are streamlined online. Invoice and payment transactions and reporting is another such example.

Summary View of Part II (Steering)

Chapters 4 to 6 have looked at three important tools for steering the ship and successfully navigating the challenges. They respectively focused on the knowledge for balancing Plan-Execution, External-Internal funding and Process-Result orientation. Together they can be visualized as a steering wheel at your disposal with key controls, as shown in Fig. 6.4.

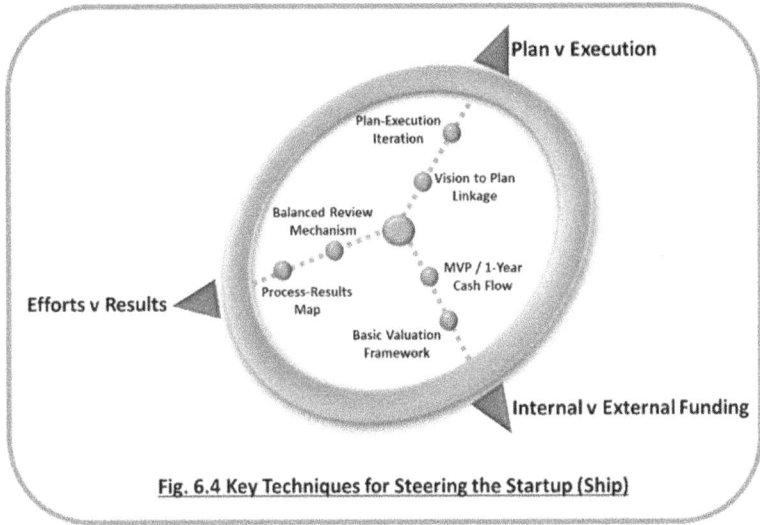

Plan v Execution

Plan-Execution
Iteration

Vision to Plan
Linkage

Balanced Review
Mechanism

MVP / 1-Year
Cash Flow

Efforts v Results

Process-Results
Map

Basic Valuation
Framework

Internal v External Funding

Fig. 6.4 Key Techniques for Steering the Startup (Ship)

Of course, steering can have a few more dimensions. In your start-up, you may discover certain unique challenges to be addressed. That knowledge will augment and create your basket of steering techniques. The three key areas covered here provide a strong foundation for this segment of start-up management and a methodology to address new decision scenarios.

All along this process, the endgame remains in focus. Its understanding, definition, and conscious efforts towards reaching there are paramount. We now move on to the first chapter of the third and final part of the book, which takes us through that phase.

Positive Bias in Balancing Acts of Steering

One more useful summary as we wrap up Part II is that the three key balancing acts of steering in the three chapters advocate striking a delicate balance between two equally important initiatives. While the mathematical midpoint of that balance would be the 50% mark, we have already indicated a slight bias for efforts over results in this chapter. Here is a combined view of those finer balancing acts in Fig. 6.5. We recommend a positive bias favoring Execution, Internal

Funding Resources, and Efforts, respectively, over Plan, External Funding, and Results. This should not be interpreted as superseding but instead as where you want to be slightly inclined while all other things are equal.

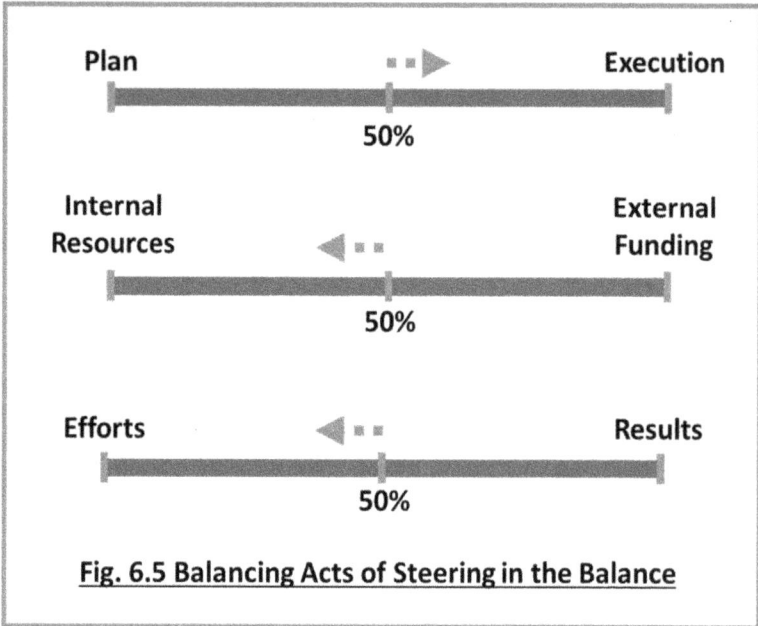

Fig. 6.5 Balancing Acts of Steering in the Balance

Useful Reference from Ittiam Experience

From my Ittiam experience, we will add useful references to this chapter's focus on balancing process efforts and result orientation.

At Ittiam, we were clear from very early in the journey that the key to successful results is the underlying competency of the people and technological innovation. To address this combined set of areas, one of the processes we have instituted is recognition of people's excellence along the "technical ladder," in addition to conventional career growth along engineering and management ladders.

An overview of this technical recognition process at Ittiam is depicted in Fig. 6.6.

BALANCING PROCESS EFFORTS AND RESULT ORIENTATION

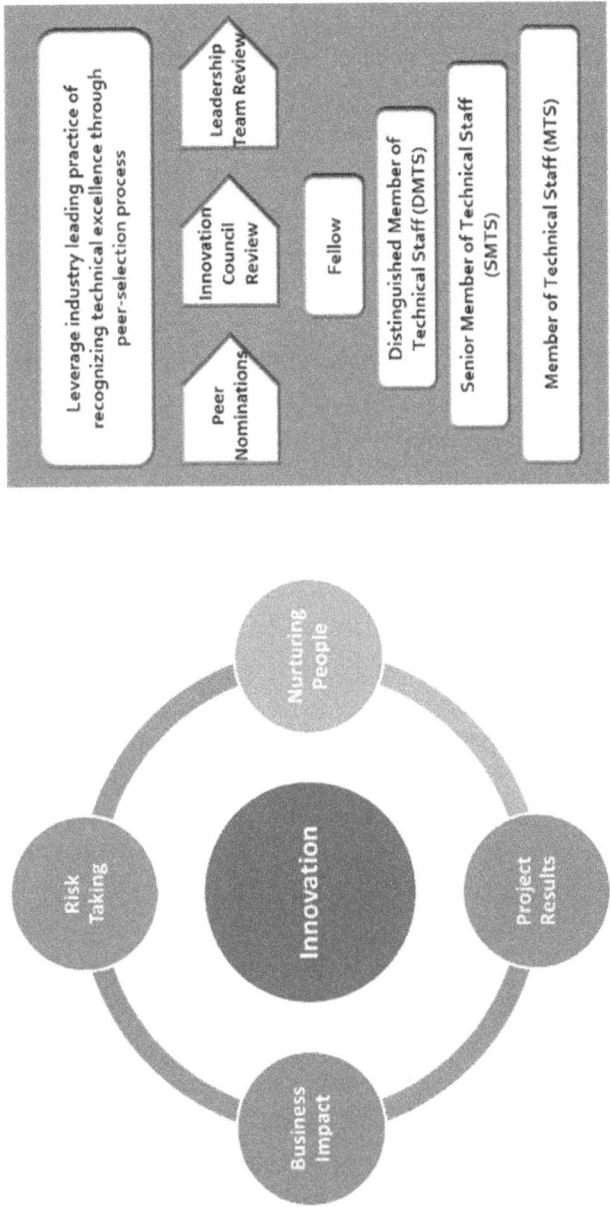

Fig. 6.6 Ittiam Technical Recognition Process – Competency, Innovation, Impact and Guidance of People

As conveyed in Fig. 6.6., Ittiam's technical ladder recognition process is modeled along the industry-leading practice that IEEE

81

(Institute of Electrical and Electronics Engineers) follows in recognizing technical excellence through a *peer-selection process*. Peer-selection brings a unique value to the process for two reasons: a) When technologists receive appreciation from different quarters, they are most excited about the appreciation coming from their professional peers and b) The feedback from peers is typically out of true appreciation of class and excellence and does not carry any expectation in return - the peers can also provide this feedback anonymously. The recognition is awarded for exceptional technical leadership, providing a strong competitive advantage to Ittiam's current and future technology offerings. Competitive advantage, in turn, is achieved through innovations in product development and fostering a culture of technical excellence.

By institutionalizing this process, we have brought the inner layers of people and processes to the fore to provide visibility, recognition, and motivation.

Top Three Takeaways (T3)

1. Process and Result focus are both necessary. They are like two sides of the same coin. The mathematical probability for each is 50% in a coin toss event. If a start-up has a slight bias, we recommend that process orientation be slightly more emphasized.

2. Start-up organizations must establish a clear framework to review progress on both the vectors and balance the reward mechanism.

3. The review framework presented in this chapter provides a basic template to document all the key processes, identify the map that links processes to key result areas, and establish a well-balanced review mechanism for teams and individuals. It is vitally important that the leadership prioritizes progress on both dimensions and communicates that priority to everyone.

It is common to see individuals and teams appreciated and criticized based on the results produced.

Process efforts are likely silent but no less important.

A Light-Bulb Moment in Chapter-6

7

Understanding the End Game Options

Start-ups typically explore numerous paths but must understand that only a few steady-state options serve as home.

Let us start this chapter with an easy 5-question trivia that you should be able to crack quickly. You are required to name the start-ups based on the descriptions given. This is intended not to test your knowledge of the tech industry but to grasp and understand the excellent representative evolution of start-ups toward their homes. The trivia answers are given in Fig.7. 1.

1. The start-up, co-founded in 1975 by Steve Allen and his more famous partner and globally renowned business icon, became successful and made its IPO (Initial Public Offering) in 1986. It has since remained one of our most relevant technology companies. It has been among the top-5 highest-valued (measured through Market Capitalization or Market Cap) companies worldwide for several consecutive decades.

    It is _____.

2. Jim Clark and Marc Andreessen founded the start-up in 1994 for web browsing, which soon became dominant. However, it lost out to its competitor product, Internet Explorer, from Microsoft and has since been disbanded.

   It is _____.

3. The start-up founded by Rod Canion, Jim Harris, and Bill Murto in 1982 became the largest supplier of Personal Computer Systems in the 1990s. It made its IPO in 1983. However, due to market forces and consolidation, it merged with Hewlett Packard (HP) in 2002 and has since operated within the HP fold.

   It is _____.

4. The start-up founded by Andy Rubin in 2003 to develop operating systems for Digital Cameras and Smartphones was acquired by Google in 2005. Since then, it has been working as an internal product offering of Google. It has become the most extensive operating system running over 5 billion devices worldwide, including Smartphones, Smart Watches, and Cars.

   It is _____.

5. The start-up, founded by Brian Acton and Jan Koum in 2009, soon became the world's most popular and free-of-cost messaging and voice calling application on the internet. Facebook acquired it in 2014, and since then, it has been operating as an offering by Facebook (Meta), retaining its original brand name.

   It is _____.

Question	Answer
1	Microsoft
2	Netscape Communications
3	Compaq
4	Android
5	WhatsApp

Fig. 7.1: Startup Trivia Answers

Outside of the visible stories, hugely successful and not-so-successful, illustrated above, hundreds and thousands of not-remembered start-ups have completely failed, closed, and been forgotten. **They are nameless.**

A new start-up must think from the beginning and keep thinking throughout its journey, "How would it like to be remembered and recorded in history"?

Infinite Space of Creativity Maps onto a Finite Set of Models

While thousands of movies are made every year, and the global entertainment industry has been growing into a behemoth of value and impact, the entire gamut of movies made in the world falls into a few basic genres such as Action, Comedy, Drama, Fantasy, Horror, Mystery, Romance, Sci-Fi and Thriller.

Again, regarding how well the movies are remembered, there are a few basic categories, such as Award-Winning, Box-Office Hit, Blockbuster, Critically Acclaimed, Commercial Flop, and People's Choice.

In a not-so-dissimilar manner, start-ups belong to a shortlist of industry clusters such as e-commerce, healthcare, hi-tech software, or electric vehicles. Depending on their progress, the start-ups would find a home that can fall into one of the short descriptions below:

1. Successful Public Company
2. Successful Private Company
3. Successful Merger with Another Company
4. Successful Acquisition by Another Company
5. Sustained Success Under Different Corporate Umbrella
6. Loss-Making Rapidly Growing
7. Once Dominant, Now Defunct
8. Sick and Bankrupt

Taking a cue from the entertainment industry genres and the home models that start-ups may map onto, it seems reasonable to suggest that one should think about the type of home they would like to reach from the beginning of their start-up. This is just as important as the type of start-up one wants to build, towards which extensive thought process and efforts are committed upfront.

Visualize Living in the Home Descriptions for Your Start-up and Its Stakeholders

Let us do a thought experiment on what some of the home descriptions as mentioned above mean from a start-up perspective. This is not an exhaustive view of all the descriptions but a sampling to get a close feel of what it would feel to be in the described positions.

Let us pick the two cases of a Successful Public Company and a Loss-Making yet Rapidly Growing Company. The former has many real-world examples to study and understand. The latter may indicate negative aspects because it is loss-making, but it can also involve many positive aspects in its overall strategy. A few modern business models focus on rapid growth and customer base expansion at the implied risk of losing money.

Think how you would feel about your start-up having grown successfully and become a public company. It brings excellent visibility, recognition, and a sense of achievement.

UNDERSTANDING THE END GAME OPTIONS

On the other hand, such companies are under relentless pressure to show revenue and profit growth every quarter, year after year. It's a different world to be under the constant and rigorous scrutiny of the stock market, investors, and analysts. Your founding team, management team, and you will all have to evolve, transition, and even disappear. Taking a holistic view, if your visualization shows you to be in the happiest place in such a world, it will be a significant home option to consider.

Now to visualize the next case of loss-making scenario. If it is due to poor performance and fundamental business issues, it is undesirable and you would want to get out of it immediately. Let us keep that scenario aside for a moment. Instead, as mentioned, there are a few modern business models where investors encourage rapid growth and are willing to fund it even at the cost of making a loss in the short term. Your start-up could be becoming very popular and visible, serving tens of millions of consumers and households with excellent service they love to get. This will create a great sense of achievement and satisfaction in you and your team. On the other hand, you could be living in a world of discomfort. You know the external funding supply could dry up quickly, leaving you and your team vulnerable. How would it feel to be unable to pay the salaries for your staff one fine day or to have much of the management decision-making and control dictated from outside? Taking a holistic view, if your visualization shows you are in the happiest place there, you may need to consider this home option. This is the time for you and your stakeholders to understand and reflect on the various home options.

At this stage of the book, this is all about understanding the home option. You must also ask the equally important other half of the question. Can your start-up get there, and are you tuned for it? The next chapter will look at this complementary part of the question.

Map of Start-up Qualities and End-Game Options

In parallel to the reflective exercise to understand the various home options, you can observe and study the start-ups and companies around your industry domain to identify a map of their key intrinsic qualities and their influence on the home position. For example, what are the common and prominent characteristics of start-ups that have achieved successful acquisition? Are the characteristics different from that of start-ups that have been successful while remaining private? You can document your observations from this study.

Fig. 7.2 presents an initial template to document the intrinsic qualities of the start-up and how they correspond to the endgame options. Such a map for your start-up at any given time will be quite informative to understand the realistic direction ahead. This will be a specific exercise you will undertake in the next chapter.

Intrinsic Qualities of Startup	Possible Endgame Scenarios							
Observation Map: Intrinsic Qualities and End Game Scenarios	Successful Private Company	Successful Public Company	Successful Merger	Successful Acquisition	Sustained Under Different Corporation	Loss-Making Rapidly Growing	Once Dominant Now Defunct	Sick and Bankrupt
Size of the Market Addressed by the Startup		O	O			O		
Differentiation of the Core Offerings	O	O			O		O	O
Ability to Remain in the Top Position of the Landscape			O	O			O	
Scope for Expansion and Diversification	O	O					O	
Business Model		O		O		O	O	O
Profitability Linked to Business Model	O	O	O	O	O	O		
Ability to Raise Large Capital for Growth		O	O			O		
Potential for Inorganic Growth		O	O					

Fig. 7.2: Intrinsic Qualities Map to Endgame Scenarios

Along the rows of the map in Fig. 7.2 are marked the intrinsic qualities (like the DNA) of a start-up that have a bearing on where it could aspire to reach. The columns on the map cover the eight "home descriptions" stated earlier.

The markers in the map are based on what you observe around you in your industry. They show your understanding, from the study, of endgame scenarios on which the intrinsic qualities significantly influence. For example, to be a successful public company, many attributes must be in place, as shown by the map.

We already noted in Chapter 4 the old-school virtue of profitability priority and the power and flexibility it provides to the start-up. You would see its value in real life through how that quality influences and opens doors to many endgame scenarios one would like to participate in.

Remember Fig. 7.2 only presents a template with illustrative markings, while the actual one is to be created by you through your observations for your industry domain.

Converting the Map to Self-Assessment Tool

Each start-up has certain intrinsic qualities that become leading indicators of the potential destinations ahead. For example, high-performance sports coach initially assesses an aspiring young athlete and opines that their current body structure is more suitable for success in a marathon run than a 100 meters sprint. However, if the youngster is passionate about becoming a sprint champion, different steering (diet, fitness, and training regime) must be pursued. While strategic steering can expertly guide a start-up to a newer destination, analysis of the current snapshot provides a good idea of the future potential. The observation map shown in Fig. 7.2 can be enhanced to perform this self-assessment.

To convert this map into a self-assessment tool, each cell can be marked with a "+" or "-" sign depending on whether your start-up's quality at the time of assessment is a strong positive correlation to the endgame scenario or a strong negative correlation. Then as a first-pass deduction, the scenario column with the highest entries of "+" could provide the initial indication of where the ship is poised to reach.

UNDERSTANDING THE END GAME OPTIONS

You can refine this tool more profoundly during its application. For example, markings can be graded on a scale of 1 (low correlation) to 5 (maximum correlation) instead of a simple "+" or "-. "

Such a self-assessment would be one of the key pointers to reaching a clear definition of home amongst all stakeholders, which we will discuss in the next chapter.

Where Are We?

While everyone could have come together unanimously with the start-up's purpose and dream, there may be different ambitions in stakeholders' minds and the start-up's capabilities regarding defining the best place to go.

As enumerated in this chapter, the prerequisite for creating a consensus among all the stakeholders is a clear understanding of endgame options. With that understanding in place, the logical next step is defining and agreeing on the home which is taken up in the next chapter.

Top Three Takeaways (T3)

1. There is a finite set of endgame options towards which a start-up needs to plan its future.

2. You need to visualize living through the possible home scenarios and understand where you would be happy to reside.

3. Your start-up's intrinsic qualities lend themselves to being naturally inclined toward specific endgame scenarios. A generic industry map of this relation can be created through observation and study. Taking this further, you can conduct an objective self-assessment of your start-up at any given time to help reach a clear definition of home amongst all the stakeholders.

Understand the endgame (Home) scenarios early through external study and internal discussions.

Know the Homes that your start-up's DNA points to.

A Light-Bulb Moment in Chapter-7

8

Having a Clear Definition of Home

Just as everyone co-owns the start-up's dream, every stakeholder also understands, agrees upon, and desires its home.

"The Home" fulfils the set of clear goals of the stakeholders at a given time of the start-up journey and they want to reach there. It can also be known as their preferred steady state. The founders must define the home both from their individual and start-up perspectives. The two perspectives need not be the same.

It is vital to understand that different stakeholders look out for their returns, commonly known as "exit", at different points in time of the start-up journey. The start-up must facilitate this process to function effectively. While the desire to keep going could be there, stakeholders must decide at the right time to exit and let the next enter. There can be multiple exits in a start-up's roadmap. For example, the computer giant Dell was a start-up founded in 1984 by Michael Dell, went public in 1988 to reach the first exit, and then was taken back as a Private Company in 2013. The company's rationale for going Private in 2013 was reported to be based on significant slowdown in the personal computer market on which Dell's business primarily depended. The substantial changes in the products, services and business model required to succeed in that market environment were more feasible to accomplish as a private company with a long-term strategic focus. In contrast, public companies must manage short-term quarterly forecasts, results, and stock price volatility.

The start-up can have a much longer life to grow into an institution beyond the active career span of its founding entrepreneurs and the target time window of investors.

Influencers of Home Definition

Defining the home is a democratic process. Every stakeholder influences the home definition.

Consider an investor who came on board with an investment made from a fund with four years left for its end-of-life term. Situations like this are very common. Investors coming in at the start of their fund's life term have a more extended period to play with, and vice versa when they come in at the later part of their fund's life term. Assuming you are doing this exercise of home definition in the third year of their investment, such an investor would be heavily inclined towards a home that can be reached soon. It could mean an acquisition or merger since other scenarios may not be fulfilled within the required time. Alternatively, they could consider an exit by offering their shareholding to another investor if the start-up can facilitate making that match within the time available. We will consider these cases and similar special situations later in the next section.

Next, let us put ourselves in the founders' shoes.

The founders may take a very long-term view to define the home as they may be in it for a long haul. Sometimes, even the founding team cannot be viewed as one homogeneous cluster with one common intention. Depending on the point in the career lifecycle each one is at, the preferences could vary, and a more granular view may need to be taken.

The people in the company have a strong influence as well. The environment, team culture, competencies, and career aspirations are important factors in the home definition. For example, consider a team built on in-depth expertise in certain advanced technologies for long-term research. The success criteria for research teams are defined over a longer period (say, 2-3 years) and include different metrics such as technology breakthroughs, fundamental patents, and highly cited publications. Its acquisition possibilities may be limited to fewer target companies, since the target must exclude several prospective companies focused on services, tactical project execution, and short-term revenue generation. In a talent-driven business, a home that does not meet the people's aspirations would rarely be feasible.

Finally, although it may not be apparent, the customers are also key influencers. For example, consider the case where the start-up is a significant partner for several leading companies in a market segment, some of whom may be competing with one another. In this scenario, none of those leading companies would like the start-up to be acquired by the other, affecting the competitive equilibrium. Alternatively, if the start-up is heavily dependent on one or two major customers for its business, say, more than 50% of its revenues, it is understood that the customer must first be consulted in the endgame decision.

Start-ups with an extensive customer base, say tens and hundreds, with long-term support commitment made to them, would need to find a home model where their continuity and longevity are assured first and foremost.

This section reminds us why People, Investors and Customers are the three pillars of our stakeholders' spectrum as we have considered from the very beginning of this book. They are the essential parts of the Ship (start-up) and the heavy influences of the Shore (home) it can reach.

Handling Small Diversions, Time Constraints, and Partial Exits

As mentioned in the preceding section, one of your investors may seek an early exit due to their special time constraint arising from the fund's lifecycle. A similar situation can arise with one of the co-founders due to their constraints. These cases could be handled as smaller, off-cycle, partial exits without impacting the overall vision and direction of the start-up.

The interests of people seeking interim exit must be taken care of in the best way possible, but it need not affect the big picture. Let us say the ship can have a few important stopover ports along the route, but that need not change its strategic destination, which is the aspirational state for most of its stakeholders. Two important steps in this process would be identifying the buyer or party who can provide the interim exit and facilitating a fair price for the shareholding.

As listed below, there are four possible choices for the buyer or party providing the interim exit (i.e., purchasing the shareholding):

1. Another investor who is already on board,
2. A new investor who is aligned with the vision and strategy and wants to play a key role,
3. Another member of the founding team or management team,
4. In special circumstances, the start-up itself.

Choice (1) is straightforward and seamless. The investor is already on board and part of the stakeholders' spectrum. The compatibility and alignment between the investor and start-up are already in place, leading to smooth functioning.

Choice (2) is quite feasible, but it would again require careful search and selection of the investor, considering the same principles applied initially to bring in a new investor, as discussed in this book. This will typically take a longer time than (1).

Choice (3) can work out positively for the company to reinforce peer support and keep the shareholding tighter within the team, assuming there is personal financial affordability from the person(s) buying to provide the interim exit. This speaks highly of the team culture and openness in the start-up. Time-wise, this can also work as efficiently as (1).

Choice (4) would perhaps be the last option to try. It becomes viable if the start-up performs well financially and can afford to deploy its reserves for this purpose of providing an interim exit. This process is complex as the government regulatory framework must be adhered to. The shareholders' written consent must be obtained for the start-up to buy from only a specific shareholder(s) to provide them with the interim exit. Nevertheless, it is an option to keep it in the armory. The time required for this choice would be longer than (1) or (3). It would compare with (2) regarding time needed and uncertainty involved.

Fairness of the interim exit price can be achieved through engaging independent valuation agencies, using the data from most recent investment transactions, and facilitating mutual consent between the party seeking an exit and the one ready to provide it.

Home Definition and Story of Yahoo

Let us briefly recap the story of Yahoo and Microsoft's acquisition bid for the company in 2008. That story created large waves in the industry at that time. We will not attempt to judge what happened and what could have been done better. Instead, we will look at it purely in terms of what has been reported in the public media and how we can relate the events to this chapter's focus on having a clear home definition.

Yahoo was one of the pioneers of the early internet era in the 1990s and became one of the most popular technology companies in the world. It was founded in 1994 by Jerry Yang and David Filo, graduate students of electrical engineering from Stanford University. The company's wide-ranging services introduced hundreds of million customers worldwide to email facilities, internet searches, online news, and location maps.

In 2008, Microsoft made a whopping $45 billion offer to acquire Yahoo, representing a 62 percent premium over its market value. Yahoo rejected the offer because it *"substantially undervalued Yahoo."* The deal did not go through. The general industry opinion was that it was a great offer and a highly beneficial deal for the company, its shareholders, and its customers. However, the decision think-tank at the company had a different viewpoint.

In 2017 Verizon Communications acquired the operating business of Yahoo for only around $4.8 billion, and it became part of Verizon Media Group. Then, in 2021 the private equity firm Apollo Management Group completed the acquisition of Verizon Media Group (Yahoo) for $5 billion.

The point of this story is about the key moment in 2008 when the precise definition and consensus around home definition was perhaps missing within Yahoo stakeholders' spectrum. Based on the dramatic fall of its valuation later, one can say that it was a great opportunity lost in 2008. However, let us treat this data to realize how critical it is to have a clear definition and consensus of home and the importance of listening to every stakeholder's voice.

Creating the Self-Assessment Map Introduced in the Previous Chapter

Here is a quote attributed to the Founder and Chairman of one of India's most respected start-up-turned-global software powerhouses, Infosys Limited, Mr. Narayana Murthy:

"In God, we trust, everybody else brings data to the table."

We refer to Mr. Murthy's quote now since you could be overwhelmed with many thoughts and preferences from different stakeholders and influencers of home definition. The stage is set for you to employ the self-assessment tools described in the previous chapter to take an objective view of your start-up's intrinsic qualities and map them onto possible endgame home scenarios. Fig. 8.1 provides an illustrative view of this exercise.

Here are some valuable notes and guidelines while performing this exercise.

You can do the rating as an individual, a team within your start-up, or a set of teams, including representation from investors and advisors. You can merge the data and consolidate from multiple assessments done independently.

HAVING A CLEAR DEFINITION OF HOME

1. In the current state of your start-up, mark the realistic rating of how well your start-up would enable the endgame scenario for each quality described in the rows. For example, if you address a tremendously large market opportunity (first row of quality in the table), the rating could be a 4 or 5 against a successful public company (first column of endgame scenario in the table).

2. While the structure is provided to facilitate an objective assessment, it is understood that each cell marking has an element of subjective rating by the person(s) who is doing the assessment. To support the ratings, you could ask for additional data to be presented. For example, to rate the ability to remain in the top position of the landscape, the assessor could be asked to submit independent market survey data that includes the start-up's performance.

3. The first cut of the home pointer will be the column (endgame scenario) with the highest value in the "Total" row. The second pointer would be the next highest, and so on. To freeze the fully defined pointer, you must supplement this quantitative analysis with consensus-oriented qualitative discussion amongst the stakeholders.

4. This exercise also provides all options in the preferred ranking order. In addition to the top choice, the next best choice would also be of interest in the light of the "working with the backup home option," to be discussed later here.

Mark each cell from 1 (low correlation) to 5 (max correlation) of how your startup's intrinsic quality relates to the scenario	Possible Endgame Scenarios							
	Possible Endgame Scenarios							
Observation Map: Intrinsic Qualities and End Game Scenarios	Successful Private Company	Successful Public Company	Successful Merger	Successful Acquisition	Sustained Under Different Corporation	Loss-Making Rapidly Growing	Once Dominant Now Defunct	Sick and Bankrupt
Intrinsic Qualities of Your Startup								
Size of the Market Addressed by the Startup								
Differentiation of the Core Offerings								
Ability to Remain in the Top Position of the Landscape								
Scope for Expansion and Diversification								
Business Model								
Profitability Linked to Business Model								
Ability to Raise Large Capital for Growth								
Potential for Inorganic Growth								
Total | Preliminary Pointers	N1	N2	N3	N4	N5	N6	N7	N8

Fig. 8.1: Self-Assessment Tool To Determine Home Pointers of Your Startup

HAVING A CLEAR DEFINITION OF HOME

Role of Comparator (Competitor) Companies

Typically, we don't look at competition with warmth. Is it a major disadvantage for the start-up to be in a market with many competitors?

It may not be preferable for a start-up to face many competitors, but not having any competition could be bad. Why?

When a start-up formulates its idea and business plan, not having a clear competitor or comparator would mean one of two things. Either they are onto something fundamentally new in the field, poised for a great breakthrough, or they are trying to pursue an idea that has been tested and abandoned or is too infeasible to be of any practical value. Are you the first to discover this new goldmine, or is it a barren land with nothing to be harvested?

The reason for bringing the comparator (competitor) view at this stage is that it helps with specific pointers to define the potential home. It is very instructive to understand what has happened with actual and virtual comparators to the start-up:

- Companies currently in competition and their steady-state position provide helpful pointers to where your start-up can potentially reach.
- Sometimes, the competition can virtually reside as an entity with a giant corporation. Their corporate position, the business impact they create, and the industry value they command are all valuable data points.
- There could have been comparative start-ups from history. They might have changed course, got acquired, or even closed. There is much to learn from their actual performance and track record.

Internal and External Signals

As you can see from the information shared in this chapter, defining your start-up's home can benefit from internal and external signals. The internal signs are the voices of the stakeholders. They state their constraints, preferences, and aspirations, which can then be amplified with the help of the objective self-assessment tool presented. External signals come from comparator companies. They provide the reality check.

You can use both internal and external signals proactively to define a motivational and realistic home clearly. You must strive for a consensus on this definition, giving due consideration to all the stakeholders.

With the great efforts made to reach a collective understanding of the endgame options and consensus on the home definition, steering toward home becomes a continuous and conscious process, as outlined in the next chapter.

Working with a Backup Option for Home Definition

As with all aspects of life, it is advisable to work with a backup option for home definition. This is not a sign of weakness or timidness in pursuing the goal stakeholders want to achieve. Instead, it should be seen as a realistic approach to face several uncontrollable external forces before reaching home.

The simplest backup option will be a second choice within the same endgame scenario if that is applicable. For example, the three scenarios of "Merger," "Acquisition," and "Independent Brand under a Different Corporation" all facilitate having a backup option. While keeping the type of home constant, you would want to have the first name (Plan A) and second name (Plan B) to initiate the dialog in that sequence.

Pursuing a backup option across endgame scenario types is more difficult but not impossible. For example, successful public and private company options could be considered alternatives, as both require strong differentiation, growth plans, and profitability. However, the scale requirement is much more significant for the public company. So, depending on such growth strategies, both organized and inorganic, succeeding in practice, the private company model can serve as a backup to the public company model. Under some circumstances, the merger could be a viable alternative to the public company model.

While there will be some unique situations depending on the nature of your start-up and industry, this approach provides a greater chance of a successful conclusion.

Useful Reference from Ittiam Experience

My Ittiam experience will act as a valuable reference to this chapter's focus on clearly defining home.

The home definition for Ittiam has not been static. It has evolved pragmatically over the years. However, true to the principles advocated here, the definition has always been maintained with the stakeholders' clear understanding and consensus.

During the early years of enjoying a fast growth trajectory, we were reasonable to aspire for a home as a public company. However, with a closer understanding of the markets we participate and their limitations of scale, we are realistic with the primary home definition of being a successful and influential private company. With this position providing a strong base, the continued technology impact we create and the business success we produce allow us to have backup home option where a pivot can be created through a strategic M&A (Mergers & Acquisitions) process. It is interesting to note that the strong base also allows us to experiment in newer areas and find a more scalable growth line we have not yet encountered. Hence the strength of our current base is the secret of a wider set of backup options for the future.

Top Three Takeaways (T3)

1. You need to respect the views of every stakeholder in the definition of home.

2. At different key moments in the start-up journey, proactively work with all the stakeholders to synchronize on the home

definition, perform collective assessments, and keep them all fully informed.

3. Listen to the external voice that comes from comparators and competitors. They are the leading indicators coming from external sources. They help you align the home definition with the internal stakeholders.

A start-up can have a long lifecycle during which multiple Homes (endgames) are successfully reached.

"The Home" fulfils stakeholders' desire in each phase.

A Light-Bulb Moment in Chapter-8

9

Conscious Efforts to Reaching Home

Reaching the goal, or in this case, the home, is understood and desired by everyone. However, reaching home does not happen automatically and swiftly in the path of a start-up business. The leadership must consciously steer towards it.

It is well-known that the stock market is extremely demanding of the companies listed on them. A company's outstanding performance is already accounted for in its share price today. Any future upward price movement entirely depends on further growth and newer possibilities. A company can never rest on its laurels and expect the stock price to maintain itself. Every performance issue, positive or negative, directly, and immediately affects the stock price.

Let us say that the start-up in our consideration is planning an IPO (Initial Public Offering) and aspiring to become a Public Company as it's steady-state home. This immediately means that the startup will have to achieve significant growth year on year to meet the expectations of a listed company. This would, in turn, mean operating in vast markets and having sufficient fuel in the tank (people, products, customer loyalty, facilities, resources, partnerships, competitive strengths, and capital) to keep driving growth.

Does the intrinsic nature of the start-up meet the above requirements? If not, can we proactively change its characteristics to achieve them? If that cannot be done, should we change the definition of the home itself?

Case of a World-Class Boutique Firm

Consider, for example, a start-up operating successfully in a niche market, achieving leadership positions, respect, and excellent margins. However, the market itself may be small and not scalable. The start-up can have substantial reserves for its current business scale. Still, in relative terms, its financial reserves may be too undersized to drive significant growth that would be put the start-up in a higher orbit.

This would point to the start-up leadership's priority towards being a long-term closely held private company as the home or being a successful division within a large corporation after acquisition. One need not rely on only an intuitive pointer like this but can perform a complete self-assessment as described in the previous chapter. Several stakeholders can participate in bringing individual and collective judgments to the assessment. Let us say all those exercises also point to the same destination for the start-up to remain as a closely held private company or a successful division within a large corporation. If this "home definition" arising from the assessment finds consensus among all the stakeholders, it is a good situation to be in for the start-up. However, if the collective aspirations of the stakeholders are much different to become a successful public company, then there is divergence between current reality and future aspiration. To address this major change in the desired destination, the leadership must undertake a transformational exercise.

The leadership can start working on the variables by revisiting the home definition. The variables can include identifying fundamental changes to be brought into the start-up's current profile, for example, the need to bring in new investors who align with the philosophy of the organization and can invest the significant capital requirement for an orbital shift. The start-up may need to diversify into completely new markets and product lines which require expansion of R&D, Sales, and Marketing functions. The transformation can involve a few other such major initiatives.

The key takeaway from the above example is that the start-up leadership must work on a dedicated plan and strategy to reach a consensus on the home definition and then charter the course of action to get there.

Plan and Strategy for Reaching Home

As a start-up leader, you must prepare leadership priorities and targets over a multiple-year time period towards achieving the steady state of a strategic home. The recommended period is three years.

You can document the dedicated strategy using the simple template shown in Fig. 9.1 or create a more comprehensive version. This

3-Year Timeframe in Consideration	Year 20xx to 20yy				
Definition of Home (All Stakeholders)	Model as Defined by Stakeholders Consensus (For This Example: Successful Public Company)				

Leadership Priority (Reorder and Tradeoff)	Priority Owner	Year-1 Target	Year-2 Target	Year-3 Target	Remarks
Revenue from New Products					Leadership priority to grow the revenue from new products to 50% of total revenue by year-3
Revenue from Legacy Products					
Y-o-Y Revenue Growth					Grow from current level of 12% to 35% by year-3
Engineering Headcount					To increase by 20% by year-3
Support Functions Headcount					To remain flat at current level
Productivity per Person					To increase by 50% over 3 years
Gross Profit Margin					Grow from current level of 28% to 40% by year-3
Cumulative Customer Base					Grow from current base of 200+ customers to 300+

Fig. 9.1: Strategic Priorities and Targets for Reaching Home

document is dedicated for the purpose of plan and strategy towards reaching home. It goes beyond the one-year window of annual business plans and explicitly comprehends the strategic changes and trade-offs the start-up must implement.

As you can see from the strategy template, it is customized for the "home definition." It lists the priorities established, the targets, and the remarks that will all lead to the home definition. It is essential to assign an owner for each focus and track the progress at regular intervals against targets.

For example, it is essential to reach a happy consensus among all the stakeholders about the desired home for the year 2026, say, 3-year mark starting from current year 2023. At the same time, it is also crucial to be embarked in all areas to ensure that progress toward that home happens regularly and shows a considerable shift upwards every year.

Completing the two exercises in the templates of Fig. 8.1 (definition) and Fig. 9.1 (strategic plan) gives you two critical instruments to navigate the ship to the desired shore.

Setting the Strategic Priorities and Targets for Reaching Home

The remarks in Fig. 9.1 explain what each priority intends to accomplish. However, identifying the priorities must be done thoughtfully, segregating them into two distinct situations:

- Home definition assessment matches stakeholders' consensus.
- Home definition assessment differs with stakeholders' consensus.

First, let us consider the natural and likely situation where the home pointer determined through the collective self-assessments also meets the stakeholders' complete consensus. In this situation, many of the performance parameters of the start-up would be already in line with the requirements to be achieved over the next 1 to 3 years. For example, the assessment shows that the start-up is primed for a successful acquisition, which the stakeholders also desire to accomplish. Many inherent qualities will already exist and may only require specific quantitative improvements. So, the strategic priorities and targets are directly derived from that analysis. They are fine-tuned depending on the prospect (the company that proposes to acquire the start-up) and possible additional requirements that may be linked to that prospect.

The second and more difficult situation is the stakeholders' consensus aspiring for a different home than the natural pointer coming from collective assessment. The leadership must first attempt to see if this anomaly can be rectified straightaway through constructive discussions, which is highly recommended. However, if consensus cannot be achieved, the strategic priorities and targets over the three years will be a major challenge to follow through. The start-up now needs to go back to the intrinsic qualities map to the endgame scenarios discussed in Chapter 7 and Fig. 7.2. For example, let us say the inherent quality of the start-up lacks large scale. Still, the desired endgame scenario (home) depends on achieving the large scale. The priorities could now include inorganic growth through acquisition, aggressive expansion into new markets, or a combination of both. This would, in turn, require significant additional capital and bringing new investor(s) on board. The strategic priorities and targets thus established would be much more challenging and require significantly more dedicated leadership and organizational efforts to make measurable progress and fully accomplish them.

Leadership Must Take Timely Decisions

It may sound obvious and redundant to say that leadership must make timely decisions to steer the start-up (ship) toward the home (shore). After all, isn't it supposed to be a fundamental part of their job description?

In actual practice, decision making may not always happen on time. When a start-up comes across significant new opportunities, they are typically accompanied by risk elements and unknown factors. Hence several aspects need to be considered together in reaching a decision. Based on the decision, the subsequent course of action could lead to success or failure. Hence the decision makers should be prepared to make themselves accountable for their decision and willing to accept the consequences to the start-up and to them individually. Despite these complexities involved in decision making, leadership must be decisive as it is one of the top qualities expected of leaders. Given this, senior-level decision-making tends to be inherently a stressful process. The pressure from the possible outcomes and their impact on everyone makes a leader very anxious. Often, all the required information may not be fully available to make strictly objective or data-driven decisions. In such scenarios, the general tendency is not to make decisions, leading to procrastination. Rationally, we need more time to gather adequate information or think through all the possibilities more deeply. However, sufficient progress may not be made in the additional time taken, and more importantly, the opportunity in question might have a limited time window that may expire. When decision making is not completed within the required time, the opportunity is closed in an undesirable way. If leadership can make a clear decision within the required time, either to pursue the opportunity or not, it provides the desirable closure. Let us depict this situation with the help of a flowchart shown in Fig. 9.2.

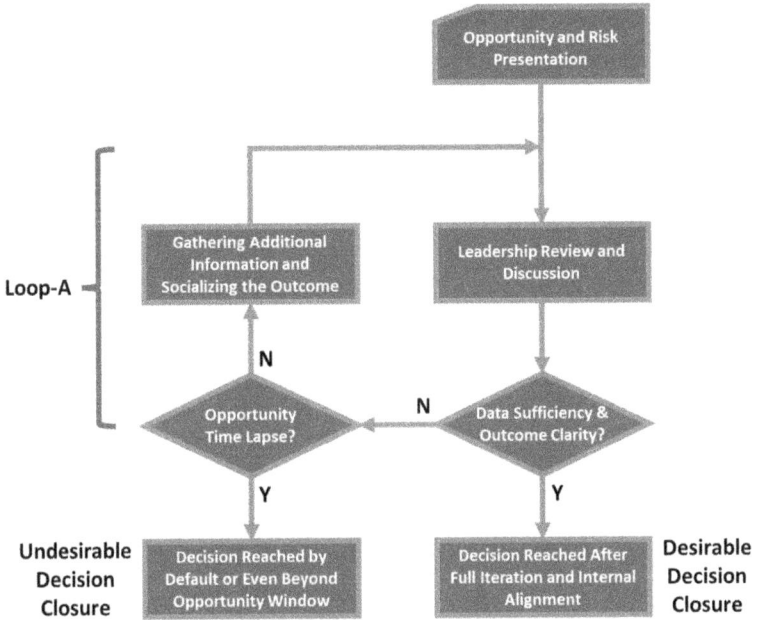

Fig. 9.2: Cost of Not Making Timely Decisions

The flowchart captures the leadership predicaments realistically. It is self-explanatory how things happen. The message is that Loop-A typically has an extended time period. The additional time taken may not be effectively used. The net result is that by the time leadership can make up their mind, it may become a default decision that the situation has already dictated, or it is too late, and the opportunity has gone away.

In summary, make your call within the opportunity window, share your rationale with all the stakeholders, and keep moving.

Even though this section appears in the final phase of the book in the context of conscious efforts to reaching home, this priority callout for timely decision-making from leadership applies to all points of the start-up journey. Consider this as having been repeated all through the book.

Surviving the Storms: Market Downturns and Economic Recessions

We will conclude this chapter with another section that has broad applicability across the start-up's lifecycle and likewise, through all the chapters of this book. The reason for placing the section in this chapter is that the strategy and actions for "Reaching Home" typically carry over multiple years. It is imperative for the start-up to have the wherewithal to fight through a period that may witness market and economic storms and be alive and well to pursue the objective of reaching the home.

Fig. 9.3: Surviving the Storms

In Ittiam's journey over two decades, we have successfully come through three major periods of severe market downturns and economic recessions. There has also been the most unexpected 2-year window of uncertainty due to pandemic in 2020 and 2021.

The key lessons learnt during these difficult periods are summarized here and the pictorial view in Fig. 9.3 helps to remember the lessons visually.

Forecast Models

The performance of a company in the recent past is usually considered a good guide to its performance in the near future. If a start-up has achieved 15% growth in two successive years, it would be quite acceptable to set a target of 20% for the next year. While this forecast model sends the correct message for everyone to work towards their goals, market downturns and economic recessions are beyond the purview of a single company's outlook. Market downturn refers to a segment specific slowdown such as in smartphones or automobiles. Economic recession is a much wider issue across the industries created by weakening of fundamental conditions such as capital availability, employment, and consumer spending.

When the forecast model sets a revenue level, all other activities, including the most important expense budget, are set in proportion to that level of revenue. The first and most direct impact of the downturn and recession is on revenue. If it starts falling in an unpredictable manner, the business can quickly go to a loss which causes a panic. Hence it serves a start-up well to typically have in the forecast model a lower band of revenue which moderates the target down for areas of revenue vulnerabilities and over-dependencies. With the help of such a model, maintaining the operating expense line close to the lower band of revenue creates a safety valve against unexpected downturns.

Deep Customer Relationships

Strategic, long-term relationships with customers are the best antidote to managing market and economic storms over a long period. These relationships take a long time to establish but they also pay back for the foreseeable future. At the heart of this relationship is the commitment for Win-Win model of both partners. Each one cares for the other's success. This model enables the start-up to understand the top priorities and issues of the customer, and design solutions and services to address them in the best possibly way. The successful track-record has been built over many cycles of collaboration. Such a foundation makes it possible for the business to continue through the storms. There may be a little downside temporarily, but future visibility continues to remain good.

Financial Reserves

It is useful to recap here a couple of key areas we studied in Chapter 5 which focused on "Balancing Internal Funding and External Venture Capital". A key takeaway was to raise external funding to the minimum level necessary. In the same breadth, the chapter also mentioned "Cash is the King" in economic recession pointing to raising capital a little more than necessary. Further, while studying the valuation equation and factors in that chapter, we saw that operating at very low cash reserve creates disproportionate impact on the start-up's valuation and volatility in its operation.

It is in a start-up's best interest to "save for a rainy day". When a start-up operates with six months of its operating expenses available in the financial reserves, it leads to some calmness. If that number can extend further to a year or more, there is absolute stability. In addition to the positive impact on the operations, a major benefit of this situation is that your mind remains strong and makes decisions in an uncluttered manner. In line with the old school virtues discussed earlier, keeping profitability in the radar allows the start-up to cumulatively strengthen its cash position over the years and be fully prepared for the downturns and recessions.

The continuity of support that the start-up brings to customers will be doubly appreciated in the downtimes. This synergizes beautifully with the lesson of "Deep Customer Relationships."

Long-Term Commitments

In difficult times, you have the opportunity to do what everyone typically does plus also a few more things to differentiate your start-up. These are a few long-term commitments that the start-up honors to distinguish itself. The first of these would be people commitment – confirmation of employment offers made on the campuses and elimination of anxiety for the existing employees about job continuity. Another of such commitment would be for high priority product development programs which are essential for success in the immediate future. We have already touched upon commitment towards customers, ensuring continuity of support and an exemplary manner of interface.

It is a natural cycle that economic downturn is followed by an upturn. When the latter happens, you want your start-up to be in the best position to capitalize on it by fulfilling the long-term commitments through the ups and downs.

Top Three Takeaways (T3)

1. Successful endings do not just happen by themselves. They are engineered with excellent planning, meticulous execution, and timely decision-making.

2. The start-up needs adequate leadership bandwidth committed to this ongoing activity of strategic importance.

3. For your start-up at this given time, identify the critical leadership priorities, owners, and 3-year targets comprising the strategic action plan for reaching home. The consensus home definition exercise from the previous chapter would have preceded this. With the two exercises in templates of Fig. 8.1 (definition) and Fig. 9.1 (strategic plan), you have two critical instruments to navigate the ship to the desired shore.

Reaching Home needs dedicated owners and efforts.

Given a start-up's characteristics, some Homes are natural to reach, and others require a transformation.

A Light-Bulb Moment in Chapter-9

10

View from the Lighthouse

Let us imagine ourselves at the vantage point of the symbolic lighthouse of the start-up ocean. The ships and vessels are spread out in the expansive waters. The observations are quite enlightening, and we can learn much from this hypothetical situation. Along with these metaphorical observations, we also describe how they correspond to the start-up world.

1. **Happy Camp:** There is a lot of activity and enthusiasm in the vessels set out on their expedition, as well as the ones that have just returned to the port. They look similar from a distance. Wait... let us take a closer look...
   The former is experiencing excitement and expectation, whereas the latter is celebrating and congratulating one another.

   In the start-up world, there is a lot of happiness and excitement when the journey begins. Similarly, those who have successfully completed the mission are understandably elated.

2. **Champions:** Some who have successfully returned are contemplating setting sail again. After all, there is no life without a voyage for a sailor. They are considering possibly going on a journey again after gaining confidence and satisfaction from the previously accomplished mission. They know they can do it again, and they have the urge to do it again. They may do it on the same vessel or build something new.

History of start-ups shows some entrepreneurs taking their learning and success from one venture to the next. Some continue to work together again and others partner with new team members. Confidence and excitement become contagious.

3. **People on Course:** Further out in the ocean, a few vessels are cruising at a certain speed and moving towards a direction purposefully. The people on board sound clear and look cheerful. They still have miles to go, but they know what they are doing and are confident of reaching their destination.

Some start-ups stand out through the clarity of their vision and confidence. They exhibit these characteristics very early and through the course. When you speak with them, you know they are headed for success. In the context of this book, these start-ups have built a solid Ship (Part I) and are expertly performing the Steering (Part II).

4. **Wanderers:** A significant number of other vessels are meandering. There is a lot of activity in them too, but it sounds chaotic. People communicate on these vessels also, but there is no conversation, only arguments, and frustration. These vessels appear to have run into a few specific types of trouble as described further in the next five snapshots.

5. **Short on Fuel:** The captain and the crew estimate that they have wasted too much effort and cannot hope to reach the desired destination with the available resources.

Start-ups running out of cash is one of the most common reasons for failure. When they hit business discontinuity, it is virtually impossible to get back on course. In the context of this book, they may have insufficient support from the Investors (Chapter 2) or have not Balanced the Funding Requirements (Chapter 5) correctly. They may have also not focused well on solving customer problems (Chapter 3) leading to unpredictable revenues and financial losses.

6. **Confused about Destination:** The stakeholders on board have strong conflicting opinions of where they want to reach. This results in arguments, mistrust, and a lack of support for one another.

Start-ups getting pulled in multiple conflicting directions is a dangerous situation that can lead to a collapse. Conflicts could arise between the key stakeholders of People, Investors and Customers. Sometimes, consensus could be lacking within one stakeholder set such as the different investors having different priorities for the long-term. In the context of this book, these issues relate directly to the important principles of understanding, defining, and reaching the Home or Shore (Part III).

7. **Virtual Standstill:** The vessel is not sailing due to unexplainable reasons. Resources are present, and everyone on board is trying hard to work things out. The reason for this stagnation could be because of missing special skills or because of a lack of coordination. Hours and days go by without a fundamental change in their position.

Sometimes start-ups get into saturation. There is virtually no change or growth when viewed through the lens of new products, customers, talent, revenue, or branding. While start-up is surviving, it is not moving anywhere towards the desired home. For the time being this may be okay, but soon the people involved lose motivation. Lack of strategy, inertia and risk-aversion are typically at the root cause of this situation. Accordingly, infusion of new strategy, talent and investor drive would be required to get things moving again.

8. **Signaling SOS:** People on board are unhappy and scared. Instead of working together closely on their present journey, they are doubting the satisfaction and fulfilment their role provides them in this vessel. They want to jump out of the ship and are attempting to escape and find refuge somewhere else.

   Continuous exodus of stakeholders (people attrition, investors exit and customer losses) from the start-up is a clear sign of crisis and the likely approaching of premature end. Recovering from this situation calls for powerful leadership decisions and swift actions taken on war footing. In the context of this book, the situation corresponds to weakness on all the three fronts – unstable Ship (Part I), uncontrolled Steering (Part II) and uncoordinated efforts to reach Home (Part III).

9. **Mid-Course Corrections:** Importantly, among the wanderers, we notice a few exceptional vessels where the Captain and the Crew are taking innovative steps to change the course. They are proactive and communicate harmoniously with everyone on board and external agencies. They are charting out a modified route. There is visible action and emerging optimism. They believe they can see the horizon.

   Start-ups in "turnaround mode" exhibit this positive change even in the overall troubled environment of underperformance. The good news is that there is belief in the team, proactive initiatives from the leadership and support from all people concerned. These ingredients point to a potential success ahead with the new strategy and roadmap towards progress.

The lighthouse view makes it evident which vessels we would like to be a part of. We would love to be the *Champions*, and if not already there, we would like to be the *People on Course*, who are on the right path to becoming champions. It's a privilege to be in the *Happy Camp* either starting an exciting new adventure or returning from one. In any case, where we don't want to be is crystal clear – *Wanderers*, being stuck with troubles in the middle of the vast ocean without innovative ideas to change the course and unable to reach the desired location.

While we notice that many of the *Champions* are doing everything right from the moment they set sail, **some have expertly navigated out of trouble** through *Mid-Course Corrections* and reached their desired destination. The Champions demonstrate the ideal solution achievable. The other set of people are also impressive as they display the *Spirit of Tennis* (described in the Preface) to triumph out of any given position.

It is very much within the entrepreneurs to make their journey to be the one that they originally dreamt of and onboarded other stakeholders. To achieve that, they need to totally commit to the required priority, focus, and hard work, and be willing to adapt themselves to take everyone to the desired home.

You will face many difficult situations in a start-up.

Believe you can reach your goal from every situation by doing things right from thereon *("Spirit of Tennis").*

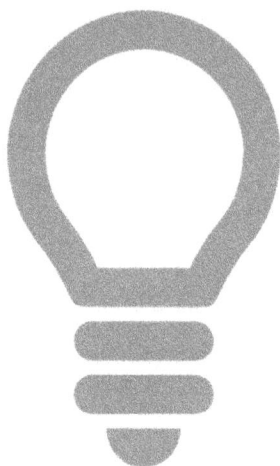

A Light-Bulb Moment in Chapter-10

Conclusion

The world of start-ups is rich with real-life stories of entrepreneurs making critical decisions on a regular basis. Some decisions look perfectly timed, while others might look like greatly missed opportunities leading to a catastrophe. Of course, looking back at a case with the benefit of knowing what happened later, one could easily understand what should have been done in the past. The key question is how one can be best guided in this journey in real-time as things are happening and how to respond best when faced with critical decision-making towards the unknown future.

Initially, with all the excitement of a start-up, an entrepreneur or a captain may want to explore many waters, but the captain must guide the ship to its desired home first. It is a priority to know your purpose and your goal. Hence one should not be taking their eyes off the prize or, in this case, the home.

Formula One Racing is among the highest-risk sports that can lead to disaster if the racers are NOT conditioned and trained. However, for those who have been trained and conditioned, it's a challenge that they overcome time and again. A start-up ensuring a successful conclusion, and professional excellence, against long odds (dynamics) of markets and economics is like winning the Grand Prix in an F1 race.

It is within the start-up leader to function at a level that will output a greater chance of success. Steering the Ship to the Shore is about doing that. It deals with the Start-up (Ship), Leadership (Steering), and Home (Shore). The definition of success or reaching home must be collectively understood and committed to by everyone involved (the stakeholders) in the start-up. This helps establish, manage, and track dedicated strategic priorities.

Hence, with the help of the knowledge you have gained through this book, you are empowered with the following three strategic actions in your armoury:

- Create the framework of the "Ship - Start-up" to establish a fuller understanding of the stakeholders and principles of operation.
- Adopt the principles of "Steering the Ship – Leadership" to best balance the journey.
- Keep on the radar "The Shore - Home" as a live guide to define the steady state that satisfies everyone on board and proactively work towards getting there.

Therefore, even if you are already in your start-up journey, there is still time to pick up this book and get valuable insights. Or if you are just commencing or thinking about the exciting possibilities of starting a venture, it's perhaps the best time to come across this book.

I wish you the very best in your entrepreneurial journey. I would like to leave you with five questions that young engineers and aspiring entrepreneurs have most frequently asked me along with my answers.

Most Frequent Questions from Youngsters and My Answers

All the questions here are important and deep. They do not have particularly right or proven answers. Please treat my responses as the best insight I can share from my Ittiam experience.

1. When should I start up? | What is the best time to start up?

The simple answer is you can start any time when you are ready. You should not worry about external factors such as the economic environment and market sentiment. It is all internal about whether you have done the preparation and are confident.

The reason is that the external environment is cyclical, and one cannot time it. It is interesting to note that Ittiam started in the worst downturn at the beginning of this century. It helped us to attract great talent since the job market was weak. Further, in the initial couple of years, we focused on deep technology development rather than business development and sales, so it worked out fine.

Any day is a good day for you to make the call.

2.   How does start up affect personal life?

Again, the simple answer is it does profoundly affect your personal life. It curtails the time you can allocate to family due to long and unpredictable work hours, travel, and the sheer mindshare. Your lifestyle and financial affordability could come down. Your friends and family may have a lot of expectations around your start-up which can add to your stress.

All the above will pale in comparison if your purpose is clear and strong (refer Chapter 1). You may no longer care about those aspects since your mind is set on a higher goal.

3.   Who should I start up with?

You should team up with people who you trust. You will have your future in the hands of the other co-founders and vice versa. Hence TRUST is the number one criterion.

After passing the most important gate of Trust, you should look to team up with people who bring complementary skills. For example, if you are technically outstanding, you need great partners in other key areas. A solid start-up requires technology, talent, engineering, business, finance, legal, sales and marketing skills. You would want your founding team to cover as much of this breadth as possible.

4. How to set up company culture?

A start-up needs a Champion Leader to define, demonstrate, communicate, and implement the company culture. The leader must be from the founding team itself, preferably the CEO, CTO, or other top-level leader. They will work closely within the leadership team to set up the culture, ethos, and principles, and take them further through the organization.

When Ittiam started, our co-founder and Head of Engineering, Mr. Sattam DasGupta (refer photo in the book's acknowledgement section) took up this responsibility and executed it to perfection. Till date, the principles live through the organization. Ittiam's culture is appreciated and respected by everyone associated with the company in any capacity.

5. How can I prepare for a real-world investor conversation?

This is a good question because it may not be possible to be 100% prepared for real-world investor conversations, although sufficient professional and systematic groundwork can be done. Please refer to the concepts and illustrations shared in Chapters 2 and 5 of the book which help with the groundwork.

You can experience close-to-real investor conversations, start-up pitches, investment assessments and feedback in television shows such as Shark Tank.

Please remember that your start-up is unique and the investor you will be speaking to is also unique. That is, both parties have specific and customized requirements and will bring up a few discussion scenarios that have not been thought about.

A few key recommendations that I would like to re-emphasize are:
1) Treat it as a meeting of two equals, viz., Yourself (Entrepreneur) and Investor.
2) Be honest and open.
3) Clearly articulate the exact differentiation and value that your venture brings to the market and the investor.

CONCLUSION

Finally, never feel disappointed about an investor rejection. You can try ten of them and need to succeed with just one. A good idea will surely find an investor whose ideology matches yours.

SRINI RAJAM

Alphabetical List of Key Terminologies and Page References

ABOUT THE AUTHOR

Srini Rajam, Co-Founder, Chairman, and CEO, Ittiam Systems

Srini Rajam is a recipient of the Distinguished Alumnus Award of the Indian Institute of Science (IISc) in the year 2013. He graduated with a Master's in Computer Science from IISc in 1984.

Srini co-founded Ittiam Systems in 2001, along with a team of senior leaders from the technology industry. Ittiam's solutions are at the heart of tens of millions of lifestyle products that drive digital media creation, consumption, and sharing. Ittiam has been ranked World's Most Preferred DSP IP Supplier by Forward Concepts for four successive years from 2004 to 2008. Ittiam is a Red Herring 100 Asia Winner in 2005 and 2013 and received the NASSCOM India IT Innovation Award in 2007.

Prior to Ittiam, Srini was the Managing Director of Texas Instruments (TI) India during 1995-2000. He led TI India to be among the most valuable R&D centers for TI. He had also served as the Chairman of the TI Asia Technical Council, and as a member of the TI Asia Leadership Team.

Srini has served as a member of the Governing Council of India's Department of Electronics Software Technology Parks (1997), as the Chairman of Indo American Chamber of Commerce, Karnataka Branch (2000), and as a member of the Karnataka State IT Task Force (2000).

SRINI RAJAM

During 2014-18, Srini functioned as an Independent Director on the Board of EdgeVerve Systems, a wholly owned subsidiary of Infosys Limited, which focuses on software products.

www.ingramcontent.com/pod-product-compliance
Lightning Source LLC
Chambersburg PA
CBHW030514100426
42813CB00001B/41